The Right Job for You

THE FUTURE OF WORK

The Right Job for You

DENNIS MARK

MICHAEL DAM

Marshall Cavendish
Business

© 2023 Dennis Mark and Michael Dam

Published in 2023 by Marshall Cavendish Business
An imprint of Marshall Cavendish International

Other Marshall Cavendish Offices:
Marshall Cavendish Corporation, 800 Westchester Ave, Suite N-641, Rye Brook, NY 10573, USA • Marshall Cavendish International (Thailand) Co Ltd, 253 Asoke, 16th Floor, Sukhumvit 21 Road, Klongtoey Nua, Wattana, Bangkok 10110, Thailand • Marshall Cavendish (Malaysia) Sdn Bhd, Times Subang, Lot 46, Subang Hi-Tech Industrial Park, Batu Tiga, 40000 Shah Alam, Selangor Darul Ehsan, Malaysia

Marshall Cavendish is a registered trademark of Times Publishing Limited

National Library Board, Singapore Cataloguing in Publication Data
Name(s): Mark, Dennis. | Dam, Michael, author.
Title: The right job for you / Dennis Mark, Michael Dam
Other Title(s): Future of work.
Description: Singapore : Marshall Cavendish Business, 2023.
Identifier(s): ISBN 978-981-5113-79-2 (paperback)
Subject(s): LCSH: Job hunting. | Career development. | Vocational guidance.
Classification: DDC 650.14--dc23

Printed in Singapore

Contents

WELCOME TO THE FUTURE OF WORK

In the new world of work, old jobs are being disrupted or eliminated just as new ones are being invented that never existed before. On top of that, professionals are not only changing jobs, but even changing careers over the course of their working life.

Here is a timely and much-needed guide to finding – and securing – the job opportunities that will bring you financial and personal fulfilment in this highly fluid business landscape. From exploring the roles most suited to your skillsets, to crafting the strategies for landing a coveted position, *The Right Job For You* will set you up for success!

The Future of Work is a game-changing collection of business books that explore the rapidly evolving landscape of work today. Within the next five years, many jobs will disappear, many will be created, but what is certain is that all will change. The titles in this new series, written by some of the most influential business leaders, thought leaders, practitioners and consultants in the industry, cover everything from business trends and technological innovations, to revolutions in work culture and the critical skills you'll need in order to stay ahead of the curve.

How to Network

Networking sources

Past experiences crossed paths
- Classmates
- College alumni
- Co-workers
- Professionals connected to your company

Associations
- Industry organizations
- Industry players/competitors
- Headhunters/recruiting firms
- Friends, family members, neighbours, social groups

Ways to develop

Use social networking tools
- Build profile/personal brand
- Connect for sharing and updates

Stay in touch with co-workers
- Common interest groups

Attend industry events
- Connect with interest groups
- Re-establish contacts

Attend social outings

How to Build, Maintain and Grow Your Network

In today's world, professionals change not only jobs but also careers. In the era of global business and interactions, we are living in a small world. People we went to school with can be our co-workers. People from a company we had dealings with previously are now our peers in the same company. Our competitors from other companies are now our partners. In the fluid world of business, networking is a must. Our network can be instrumental in providing support and a boost to our career. They can be valuable resources and avenues for professional and career opportunities. In this chapter, I'll address a variety of ways to build, maintain and grow your network.

NETWORKING SOURCES

- **Classmates**. People we went to school with are a great resource. As you and your classmates go different ways after graduating, you will likely find yourselves based in different locations throughout the world. While in school, get to know as many of your classmates as you can and let them get to know you. And keep in touch. Fifteen years after graduating from my MBA programme, a classmate and I met and discussed a business idea which resulted in the creation of a business partnership that's still going strong ten years later. You never know who you may end up working with or getting a great opportunity from.

- **College alumni**. All schools maintain an extensive list of alumni. While fundraising is a major purpose, it's also a way for alumni to stay in touch, share information and provide assistance to each other. Alumni live and work throughout the world and are a good source to identify potential career and job opportunities. An easy way to stay connected is to register in the alumni directory and include your personal and career profile for people to view. Your university's regular networking events such as social get-togethers, anniversaries, recruitment and fundraisers are great opportunities to maintain and grow your contact list.

- **Co-workers**. These include people you're currently working with and those you've worked with in the past. If you have developed a good working relationship with them, gained credibility and earned their trust, they're fantastic resources for finding out and getting potential opportunities. They can be great references and even better, give you endorsements. As with our classmates and school alumni, it's important to maintain contact with them when you or they leave the company. If you can't get together for coffee from time to time, a simple way to keep in touch is sending a hello greeting to let them know you have them in mind. Periodically posting on your social networks is also a good way to stay connected. There have been several times in my career where I was recruited by a former co-worker, and vice versa.

A valuable venue for co-worker networking is the training sessions within your organization. It's particularly important to reach beyond your usual working peers, across functional teams' boundaries. When I conducted various company in-house trainings, we consciously placed cross-functional teams together on projects. These arrangements were meant to forge relationships across broader organizational teams, especially for remote teams coming together on projects. As a faculty member, I use these occasions to spot potential talents, especially for leadership in multi-functional areas. So, don't treat it as just another training session. Make yourself stand out.

- **Professionals connected to your company**. These include suppliers, partners, service providers or contractors you work with on behalf of your company. A supplier could be a company that provides your company components to build products or packaging materials to ship your products in. Service providers could be consulting companies who provide consultation on different projects in a variety of areas. Your company hires contractors to perform specific tasks.

As you work with these partners, follow the same working principle: develop and maintain a good working relationship with them. They are a good resource for future opportunities because they tend to have a lot of visibility of the industry and know many key players. My colleagues have received job offers from these partners as well as recruited them to join our company.

One other source to keep in mind is your competitors. In today's world, a competitor today could be a partner or peer tomorrow. It's not uncommon for people to switch companies and go to work for a competitor. These people can provide valuable information about job opportunities, insight about the company and in many cases, actively recruit people from their previous company to join them.

If you are working in sales, marketing or any external-facing position, there would be many opportunities to build close relationships with your customers. These engagements help you develop a deeper understanding in the business professional context but also often help develop close customer relationships at a personal level. I have personally made great connections with many of my customers and business associates, many of whom became my most loyal customers and partners. These contacts are helpful in understanding the various job opportunities across many industries and they could be the first to recommend you for a suitable role in their company or to your competitors.

- **Industry organizations**. If you have industry organizations in your field of work – such as the IEEE
  for electrical engineers, Association of Finance and
  Accounting for accounting and finance professionals,
  or the Marketing Association for marketing professionals – consider joining them. You get useful news
  and information specific to your field through website
  postings, newsletters and magazines, as well as exposure to job and career opportunities. Make an effort
  to attend the periodic events organized by the association; these are excellent networking opportunities.

- **Job recruiters**. Throughout your career, you may
  receive calls or emails trying to recruit you for one or
  more job opportunities. Recruiters are hired by their
  client companies to find qualified candidates. The
  service they provide includes identifying, recruiting,
  interviewing and selecting qualified candidates for
  various positions. They typically get paid by successful
  hires or by qualified candidates. You will see them at
  industry seminars, conferences and other networking
  events, as well as on popular professional sites such
  as LinkedIn. Introduce yourself and get their contact
  information. Even if you don't want to leave your
  company, keep in touch with them as they are a great
  resource to provide you an up-to-date picture of the
  market.

- **Friends, family members, neighbours and social
  groups**. Last but not least, these could be the best
  ways to find out about new opportunities and to help

you find the right job. These people know you well, have a close relationship with you, share common hobbies or values, and would likely be more than willing to help. They probably also have their own network of contacts they can tap into to give you visibility to even more people. When I graduated from college, I gave my sister my resume. Within two weeks, I received a phone interview from Honeywell Inc., a multinational high-tech company. They flew me in for interviews and by the end of the day, I received offers from three different divisions. My sister was a member of a social club and through her friends there, she found out this opportunity from someone working at Honeywell at the time.

WAYS TO BUILD, MAINTAIN AND GROW YOUR NETWORK

- **Use your social networking tools**. There are a number of popular social networking and professional sites such as LinkedIn that provide a forum for professionals to communicate and share information. You should join and invite people to join you. Include your personal and professional profile in your account. You can find useful news and information shared by other people as well as job openings through these sites. You can also communicate with a vast number of people about your job interests or career opportunities you want to research.

- **Stay in touch with your co-workers**. As discussed earlier, co-workers are a fantastic resource. Having them join your social networking group is a good start, but don't forget to have face-to-face, direct contact with them if possible. In the age of digital communications, we tend to forget the importance of this. Remember that nothing creates a deeper connection than face-to-face interaction. Try to find time, once every three months or so, to have lunch or coffee. I also know co-workers who have common hobbies that draw them together. For instance, people who like to ride their bike would get together for bike runs on the weekends. The group expands as more people join, and this presents a good way to grow your network.

- **Attend industry seminars and conferences**. These events are typically organized by industry groups or by major consulting firms to have a gathering of professional people in similar fields. In the high-tech industry, big consulting services firms such as IDC or Gartner group typically have at least one major event a year to discuss and share industry news and trends and to network. Of course, their goal is also to offer their consulting services to potential client companies. Since these events tend to draw hundreds or even thousands of professionals from different companies, they present a great opportunity for you to meet with as many people as you want in one place. Over the course of my career, I have met and formed friend-ships with new people at such events and have also run into co-workers and acquaintances with whom I had lost touch.

- **Attend social outings.** Whether it's through a hobby club, sports club, or some other social organization, get-together events and social outings are good forums to stay connected and get to know people better. They allow more time for us to have longer conversations instead of the usual quick greetings and small talk at a club meeting. Through these kinds of events, I have also seen parents inquire about internship positions or potential jobs for their college children, and more often than not, they meet people who know about openings in their company or know people who are looking to hire college students.

REVERSE MENTORING OFFERS MUTUAL BENEFITS

Networking builds up your personal credibility and highlights your work profile and capabilities. Connections made through my network have helped me tap into adjacent opportunities. I have also been able to add value by connecting multiple parties to bring something to fruition. Networking is a force-multiplier, a door-opener, and in certain situations, a tipping point. An example is that of my HR leader Elizabeth, who was actively involved with Singapore universities in mentorship and business faculty classes. She was able to provide critical and relevant information to her MBA students because she was mentored by industry leaders and obtained a lot of industry knowledge from her connections.

There's a recent trend I have benefited greatly from, which young professionals should take advantage of. Reverse mentoring is a value-add in two directions for both senior and younger generations. I have learned a great deal from Millennials, GenZers and *jiulinghou* (post-90s generation), especially in fast-paced Asian economies such as China. It opened my eyes to new cultural norms and market changes. I recruited Thomas – a new-generation HR talent development expert in China – to regularly share his cross-industry learnings, such as the e-commerce market and China talent flow trends. It not only benefited the company employees but also expanded my connections and learnings from the students. As a mentor to younger executives, I firmly believe in the benefits in both directions from reverse mentoring. The younger generations have valuable first-hand experience with new evolving markets. They should seek opportunities to share their knowledge and insights with "older" management teams. And in doing this, they also build up their credibility "bank account" and strengthen their value in the network.

The Asian market's rapid growth and large young consumer segment makes this reverse mentoring ever more important for both the mentor and mentee. The younger workforce – in India and Southeast Asian countries such as Indonesia – makes up a significant market with notable consumer purchasing power and social characteristics. In particular:

- Commerce and society in these markets are fast-changing and driven by youth segment dynamics.

- Young consumers' voice and influence are magnified by their digital-native comfort level.

- For older management teams, the possibility of a generation gap within the organization could pose management challenges. Active learning within the organization is increasingly important to leverage the human capital from different age groups and experience levels. Youths should take advantage of their knowledge and familiarity of the growing market segment they represent. They could be the critical bridge from management to the market.

Wherever you are in the world, your reputation and how well you are connected are critical factors when it comes to business and professional dealings. The relationship-building journey from your networking needs time to be developed, and you should start to network as early as possible in your career.

How to Search for Job Opportunities

In today's business world, you are unlikely to stay with the same company for your entire professional career, even if you want to. Company's loyalty to employees was real at one time, but not so much now. Throughout your career, prepare to change jobs a few times, whether by choice or not. Make it a practice to keep your eyes open for better opportunities, to be proactive and take control of your career. When you want to search for job opportunities, your networking contacts are a great resource and can also be a great reference for you. The best way to get the job you want is through referrals and recommendations from people you know. These people can help you expedite the applying process by connecting you directly to the hiring manager. However, this option may not be available to you all the time. In this chapter, I will cover the different sources and ways to search for job openings.

Search for Job Opportunities

Network sources

- Classmates
- College alumni association
- Co-workers
- Professionals connected to the company
- Industry organizations
- Headhunters/recruiting firms
- Friends, family members, neighbours, social groups

Additional sources

- Target companies of interest
  - *Search their webpage for job postings*
- Professional & job search sites
- Government agency sites
- Other job posting ads, e.g. Classifieds

Additional tips

- Ready resume
- Online resources, e.g. Glassdoor
- Prepared for screening calls

JOB SEARCH USING YOUR NETWORK SOURCES

At the point you're looking for a job, hopefully you already have a significant network of contacts you've built and grown over time. Now is the time to tap into this network to help you with your job search. If you have not focused on building your network, start as soon as possible. It's better late than never.

- **Classmates.** This also includes members of school clubs, sport teams or other school organizations you joined and built relationships with. Many of them may be on social media sites such as Facebook and LinkedIn. Contact them using what you think are the most effective ways to reach them: social media, email, phone or if possible, face to face.

- **College or university alumni association**. All schools maintain an extensive list of alumni. Alumni members are encouraged to stay in touch, share information and provide assistance to each other. They present a big exposure to potential job and career opportunities all over the world. If your school's alumni have a website offering a platform for alumni to stay in touch, this would be a convenient way to let people know about your job search. Through the contact list from your college directory, you can reach out to these people as well.

- **Co-workers.** These include people you're currently working with as well as former co-workers whom you have developed good relationships with, earned their trust and gained credibility. They are a fantastic resource for finding and getting job opportunities and can also be great references for you. Your former managers are great contacts to reach out to. They obviously knew you and if they had a good working relationship with you and valued your work, they could be your meal ticket. From the companies you've worked at, you should already have a list of contacts. If you don't, you can put a list together using your phone contact list, email list, social media sites, etc. Contact them and let them know what you are looking for. If they are local, try to meet with them in person.

During a lunch outing I had with a former student, Samantha, she told me she had recently left her old company to join a financial services company. When I asked her how she got the job, Samantha told me a former colleague, who had joined this new company, recruited and recommended her. Her colleague arranged a lunch meeting for her with the hiring manager. At the end of the lunch, the manager offered her the job on the spot. Although Samantha had a good working relationship with her colleague, she did not know her well. When she left the company, Samantha asked for her contact information and kept in touch periodically. And she was very glad she did. This is not usually how the hiring process works, but it shows the power of networking.

- **Professionals connected to your company**. These include suppliers, service providers and contractors you worked with on behalf of your company, or in some cases, even your company's competitors. You should have a list of the people you had good working relationships with. They are a good resource because they have a lot of visibility of the industry and know many key players. Reach out to them via whatever avenue is most convenient and effective for them.

- **Industry organizations**. There are many professional associations in different industries, such as the IEEE for electrical engineers, the Association of Finance and Accounting for accounting and finance professionals, and the Marketing Association for marketing professionals. If you are a member, you can get useful, relevant information specific to your field through the organization website postings and newsletters. Through the website, you may also be able to post your job inquiries and have access to people in your professional field.

- **Recruiters**. Throughout your career, you will likely receive calls or email messages from recruiters trying to recruit you for job opportunities. You also find them on career and job sites such as LinkedIn. Recruiters want to add to their professional contact list and would be interested in talking to you even if they don't have any opportunity matching your interest and qualifications at the moment. In addition, they are a good source of information since they often have visibility of your industry, key companies and employment outlook.

- **Friends, family members, neighbours and social groups**. They often are the best ways to learn about opportunities and excellent resources to help you find the right job. Many of them have their own networks, so by extension, they can get your word out to many more people.

JOB SEARCH USING ADDITIONAL SOURCES

- **Companies you're interested in**. Companies post job openings as they become available. You can search on their website for job openings and submit your resume for the job you're interested in. All the openings should have a fairly detailed job description including key responsibilities and requirements. Some may list recruiter contact information but many do not. If you know someone from the company, that person can help find out the recruiter's contact information or even better yet, forward your resume to the hiring manager. Especially in a difficult employment environment, you increase your chances significantly if you can reach out directly to the hiring manager. Many companies hire contractors to handle recruiting and screening, but unfortunately, because of the high turnover rate for recruiters, your resume may fall through the cracks. It's a good idea to follow up periodically to make sure the company still has your resume on file.

- **Professional and job search sites**. There are a number of global sites as well as country or region-specific job search sites. They may have a large number of members, including professional employees, employers and headhunters. Here you can post your profile/resume. Companies also advertise and post their job openings on these sites. They provide great exposure to many job openings as well as employment contacts. From these sites, some of which offer additional features to enhance your job search but may require a premium membership fee, you can customize your search for the specific type of job you're looking for, as well as set up automatic searches to receive reports regularly. LinkedIn is an example of a job search site.

- **Classified ads** in newspapers, magazines and trade publications, including online ads. While these are not as common and popular, they still are a useful source of job opportunities.

ADDITIONAL TIPS

- Hopefully, you have been proactively managing your career on an ongoing basis, including building your network and keeping your resume up to date. If you are new in your professional life and have not built up your network, start one and keep growing it. Don't wait. If you don't have your resume or have not updated it recently, put your focus on creating the best resume possible. After all, your resume is your initial communication vehicle to potential employers. Since they will likely read your resume before deciding to interview you, don't take shortcuts in your resume writing effort. Before you start or at least during your job search, make sure you have a resume ready to go. Refer to the "How to Write a Compelling Resume" chapter for the best way to go about this.

- There are online resources such as Glassdoor.com that provide you useful information in your search for the right job and company. Information you can find includes reviews of salary compensations for specific job titles, benefits, cultures and management teams. Look to see if Glassdoor or similar websites are available in your country.

- Once you apply for a position, you may get a phone call any time. The phone call could be to set up a phone interview or it could be the interview itself. As a result, assume the phone call you get will be a screening interview and be prepared. Your success in the screening interview will get you face-to-face interviews with the hiring manager and other people in the company. You don't want to get caught unprepared for the phone interview because that might be your only one with that company. If you're not prepared, ask to schedule a time soon after so you have time to prepare.

- I saw many cases of students doing internships during their holidays. Internships are very available in Asian markets as many MNCs and local companies are tapping into younger people for ideas and energies. These are great opportunities to understand first-hand the industry as well as how well it fits with your career path. Planting your seed early as an intern also gives you exposure and a head-start for possible long-term employment with the company. I would highly recommend this as an essential pre-career starting point that all should take full advantage of.

- The growing Asian economies provide early career professionals with new potential and options on an ongoing basis. Every opportunity to serve your customers or partners should be a chance to open new doors of knowledge and to be spotted. Your customers and partners are definitely candidates for your career connections.

- The trend in Asia on switching careers across industries should be a factor to consider in broadening your connections. Success in an existing job should not exclude you from learning and exploring other areas that could utilize your current assets. My experience as a volunteer in the Red Cross exposed me to humanitarian needs and skills in saving lives, and gave me a platform to leverage my corporate world experience for a broader purpose to serve.

- You should build your personal brand, a profile that will differentiate you from the rest. This will be useful as you connect to those relevant groups of professional contacts who can endorse you. This would serve as a force multiplier.

How Companies Hire

Many college students and even professionals who have been employed for some time don't really understand how employers conduct and manage the hiring process. Understanding this process helps you better prepare for your job search, interviews and job offer negotiations. This chapter describes a typical hiring process of multinational companies in the United States. While there may be some unique differences for companies outside of US, many of them leverage the hiring process from US companies. It would be beneficial to you to do your research to understand the details of your specific company. Recruiters or Human Resources (HR) staffing managers are good places to get pertinent information. As I spoke to many HR and recruiting professionals, hiring is a challenging task, especially in Asia. With business growth and talent gaps, HR teams are under time pressure to hire strong candidates. By understanding the hiring process, you can make it easier for them to hire you.

How Companies Hire

Posting job openings

Staffing decision
- College hire schedule
- Quarterly operating budget
- Quarterly windows
- Hiring freeze?

1 Job description and selection criteria

2 Manager submits job positions for posting

3 Screening and interviewing

4 Hiring decision
- Narrow to final shortlist
- HR background/reference check

5 Job offer package
- Inclusive of fixed policies and negotiable terms

6 Onboarding preparation
- Base salary, sales incentives, stock incentives, sign-on bonus, etc
- Backup offers and backup candidates standing by

Public sector hiring
- Dictated by regulations
- Job postings on organization's website
- Submission requirements: CV with cover letter; job skill test
- Interview and hiring process (one-on-one or panel interviews)

HOW COMPANIES CONDUCT STAFFING AND HIRING

- **Staffing decision**. Companies begin working on next year's operating plan a few months prior to the next fiscal year with the goal to have a final approved plan by the start of next fiscal year. Once approved, each department has its specific budget plan showing how many additional positions can be added for the coming year. The additional headcounts include the number of new college graduate as well as experienced hires. In the US, the new college graduate hiring process is normally completed by May, with offers extended to candidates in February or March. Because of this schedule, companies' college recruiters usually visit colleges and participate in job fair events for graduating students much earlier. The experienced hires can occur throughout the year.

  It's important to remember that the annual operating budget is subject to be revised quarterly. The number of hires for each quarter may increase or decrease, depending on the company's business performance and market conditions. An exception to this planning process happens when a manager needs to replace an employee who transitioned to another job or left the company. The appropriate management level must approve this kind of hire. One additional note: the company at any time can decide to freeze all hirings and open positions. Timing also plays an important factor and dictates the manager's hiring process. Due to fiscal calendar constraints of the end of the fiscal quarter or year, managers may be given a deadline to complete their hiring or lose their head count allocations. As a result, managers may shorten the hiring process in order to beat the deadline.

- **Posting job openings**. Once the manager knows how many additional employees to hire, they write a job description for each position. The job description includes job title, main responsibilities and qualification requirements such as college degree, number of years of experience, technical skills, etc. In addition, the job description may also list desirable qualifications. To start the process, an HR staffing recruiter meets with the hiring manager to confirm the position's job level, review criteria for selecting candidates, decide whether to use an external head hunter and how to proceed with the interview process. Then the hiring manager submits the job positions to be posted on the company website and on other external sites as appropriate.

- **Screening and interviewing**. The company staffing recruiter screens the resumes, verifies candidates' qualifications and sends qualified resumes to the hiring manager. The manager or recruiter conducts phone interviews to select candidates for in-person interviews. The manager also puts together an interview team consisting of people from their team and other teams who will be working with the new hire.

Regarding interview methodology, many companies use a behavioural interview method where the interviewer describes certain work scenarios and asks the candidate to respond to the situation. This is an effective method to gauge the candidate's qualities and skills. For example, if the interviewer wants to probe for teamwork ability, they may say: "Give me an example of a time you had a conflict at work with a colleague and describe how you handled it." Or if the interviewer wants to probe for problem-solving skills, they may say: "Give me an example of a complex problem you had to solve and explain how you solved it." In terms of organizing the interview team, some managers are more organized and assign a specific area for each member to probe, such as teamwork, communication, job skills and creativity. Other managers are less structured and may leave it up to the interviewers to decide how they want to conduct the session.

Some companies also have a practice of hiring for a functional area, Supply Chain for example, without focusing on any specific job. They may not have specific jobs defined yet or may want to re-organize the job positions in the organization. After the hiring process is completed, the manager places the employee in a specific job position.

- **Hiring decision**. After all the interviews are completed and feedback collected, the manager narrows the list down to a few finalists and either decides to hire one of them or brings them in for a final interview with high-level executives. Before making the final hiring decision, the manager checks out references and HR conducts background checks on the finalists. During this final stage, the manager stays in touch with the other finalists to update them on the progress and to confirm their availability and interest in joining the company.

- **Job offer package**. Once the manager decides on a candidate, the HR manager and the hiring manager put together an offer package that includes base salary, stock incentives, sign-on cash bonus, etc. Some offer items are firm per company policy while others are negotiable. The HR manager informs the candidate and sends the offer out. The candidate is given a certain number of days to formally accept or reject the offer. This period can be a few days for an experienced hire or as long as two months for college hires due to their college's job accepting policy. During this period, the candidate can ask to clarify unclear items and negotiate the offer. Since time is of the essence, the manager will push the candidate for a decision as soon as possible. The manager likely also has a backup plan in case the offer is rejected. If this happens, the manager will quickly move to make an offer to the second finalist.

- **On-board preparation**. Once the candidate accepts the formal offer, the manager will complete the necessary paperwork and take steps to prepare for the new hire's arrival. This preparation includes procuring IT equipment, setting up the employee in the company HR and IT system, as well as lining up key people for the new hire to meet.

Although companies tend to have a similar hiring framework, they may have differences in specific hiring procedures, depending on the company size and industry. Start-ups and small companies may have simpler hiring process than large employers. For example, instead of a few rounds of interview, it may take one or two, and instead of a team of several interviewers, it may just be a couple of people, including the hiring manager. The budget planning process for smaller companies may also be less formal, and managers have more discretion over when they can hire. Moreover, since smaller companies do not have a fully staffed HR department, they may outsource much of the recruiting and screening tasks to external recruiting firms. When contacted by the company recruiter, ask for information on the hiring process so you can prepare appropriately.

How to Explore Job Options

Approaches to research

- Engage recruiters on possible roles
- Connect with company insiders
- Online job banks and networking platforms, e.g. LinkedIn

Seek out ideal/best-fit jobs

- Questions to gain visibility to explore different options
- To best fit your interests and strengths
- Relevant department or organization in the company

Consider different industry positions

- Available positions best related to field of study
- Understand the match to interests and strengths

Consider different functions within organizations

- Available departments best fit career goals/interests
- Available functions: Sales, Products, Operations, etc
- Geographic territory (international/regional)

How to Explore Job Options

When you start your job search, you may be asking yourself what job you should pursue. While this is an important question, there are other key questions you need to consider as well, such as what department/organization in a company you like to work in. This chapter helps you think through these questions, and provides ways to explore your job options, so you can make the best decision for yourself.

For every college major, there are a number of different job positions where you can utilize your skills. As importantly, there could be a number of organizations within a company that have relevant positions for your college degree. When you explore the different job options and organizations in a company, get as much information and as clear a picture as you can to determine if they fit with your interests and goals.

Refer to the table that follows. For each college major, the table shows: (1) a sample list of possible organizations in a company; and (2) a sample list of job positions in each of these organizations. I'll discuss each of these in detail.

Degree	Organization	Job Position
Electrical Engineering; Computer Science	Engineering Group	Design Engineer
		Test Engineer
		QA/QC Engineer
		BIOS/Firmware Engineer
		Document/Technical Writer
	Manufacturing Operation	Production Engineer
		Process Engineer
		QC Engineer
		Test Engineer
	Technical-Customer Support Organization	Technical Marketing Eng.
		Technical Support Engineer
		Application Engineer
	Field Sales Sales Operation	Solutions Architect
		Application Engineer
		Professional Services Eng.
		Sales Engineer
Math	Finance Dept.	Finance Analyst
		Business Analyst
		Business Planner
	Corporate/Headquarters	Merger & Acquisition Mgr
		Investment Specialist
		Business Strategist
	Engineering Group, Quality Control Dept.	QC Process Specialist
		Product Quality Specialist
		Business/Cost Analyst
Finance; Accounting	Finance Dept. Corporate Finance Dept.	Finance Analyst
		Finance Reporting Manager
		Business Analyst
		Budget Analyst
	Accounting Dept.	Cost Analyst
		Business Analyst
		Accountant
	Field Sales Sales Operation	Finance Analyst
		Finance Reporting Manager
		Business Analyst
		Customer Billing Specialist

Business	Finance Dept.	Business Analyst
		Programme Manager
		Business Planner
	Marketing Organization	Business Analyst
		Programme Management Specialist
		PR/Communication Specialist
	Field Sales	Sales Support Specialist
	Sales Operation	Order Administrator
		Programme Management Specialist
		Salesperson
	Engineering Group	Project Manager
	Customer Support Operation	Business Analyst
		Customer Returns & Escalation Manager
Marketing	Marketing Organization	Programme Manager
		Marcom Specialist
		Outbound Marketing Specialist
		Marketing Event Coordinator
	Field Sales	Programme Management
	Sales Operation	Promotion/Advertising Specialist
		Event Planning Manager
		Salesperson
	Customer Support Operation	Customer Service Rep
		Event Coordinator
		Programme Manager
		Training Programme Manager
Communications	PR Dept.	Financial Analyst Liaison
		Industry Analyst Liaison
		Marketing Communication Specialist
		Programme Manager
	HR Organization	Training Programme Manager
		Department Liaison
		Employee Development Manager
		Benefit Administrator
	Marketing Organization	Marketing Event Planner
		Programme Manager
		Marcom Specialist
		Business Development Specialist
		Industry Partnership Manager

CONSIDERING DIFFERENT
JOB POSITIONS

As you begin to search for job openings in the market place, you should know all available job positions related to your college degree. You need to understand what the positions entail, the differences between them and which ones best fit your strengths and interests.

- Let's look at an engineering example from the table. For our discussion, let's assume you graduated with a Computer Science bachelor degree (BS degree). Some of the relevant job positions for this major include Software Design Engineer, Test Engineer, Quality Assurance/Quality Control Engineer, Application Engineer and Customer Support Engineer. Each of these positions has specific responsibilities. For example, the responsibilities of a Software Design Engineer include designing an overall solution for a project or a part of a project, clearly defining inputs and outputs, and writing code. On the other hand, a Test Engineer has the responsibilities to test for software bugs and any problems between the different software programmes within the project. The Software Design Engineer position normally offers a higher salary than the Test Engineer position due to the skills required. Depending on your skill level and experience, you may find one of these two Engineering positions a better fit for you.

- Let's look at another example from the table – Finance/Accounting. Similar to Engineering, there are a number of positions applicable to the Finance/ Accounting major, such as Finance Analyst, Financial Reporting Manager and Cost Accounting Specialist. These jobs have different responsibilities. One respon- sibility of a Finance Analyst is performing an ROI (Return on Investment) analysis of a project, whereas a responsibility of a Finance Reporting Manager is gathering key business results and creating a report for company management. The former requires more finance analysis skill while the latter requires the abil- ity to understand business metrics and organize data in a logical manner.

CONSIDERING DIFFERENT ORGANIZATIONS

In addition to the job positions, you should research to deter- mine which organizations in the company are best suited to your career goals and interests.

- With a Computer Science degree, there are several organizations offering job positions relevant for the degree, including Engineering, Customer Support, Sales/Field Operations and Manufacturing Opera- tions. In the Customer Support Organization, you focus on providing technical support to customers, working with customers to design specific solutions, or providing technical training and support to sales people. In addition, you generally interface more frequently with customers and salespeople than if you work in the Engineering organization. If you have an interest in the technical as well as business side and like interacting with customers, you may want to consider the Customer Support Organization.

On the other hand, if you want to be a Sales Representative in the future, you may apply to work in Sales Operations, where you will have opportunities to work closely with the sales team and have first-hand knowledge of how salespeople work with customers.

- For a Finance/Accounting major, organizations having relevant positions include Finance Department, Corporate Finance Department, Product Operations, Sales Operations and Customer Support Organization. While you may perform similar duties in these organizations, whom you work with is different. In the Finance Department within Product Operations, you interact with engineering teams, whereas you work with sales people if you're in Sales Operations. Working in Sales Operations gives you exposure to the external business world. On the other hand, working in Product Operations gives you a more in-depth view of the internal workings of the company.

One other factor to consider is which organization may offer opportunities that align with your goal. If you like to gain international experience, working in Sales Operations may present opportunities for you to work in an overseas sales office in the future.

Small and medium-sized companies may have multiple functions combined into one organization or department. For example, Technical Support is within the Engineering department. In addition, employees in smaller companies may perform more than one job function. For example, if you work in the Marketing department, your job duties may include marketing communications, product launches, sales training and public relations. If you work in the Finance department, your job duties may include business analysis, programme management and business reporting. Working in a smaller company offers you the advantage of learning and developing different skills in multiple areas, whereas you tend to develop a more specialized skill in a specific job in a big company.

When you explore the different job options and organizations in a company, get as much information and as clear a picture as you can to determine if they fit with your interests and goals.

HOW TO RESEARCH JOB POSITIONS AND ORGANIZATIONS

If you are in college, meet with as many company recruiters as you can when your school holds career/job fair events. Ask the recruiter about the different positions in the company that match your degree, to describe the different duties from one position to another, and provide you copies of the job description. In addition, talk to the recruiter about the different organizations in the company that have positions where your degree is applicable and to explain to you the differences among these organizations. Many universities also conduct tours to different companies that students may be interested in joining. Take advantage of these opportunities where you can observe first-hand and interact directly with employees and managers These are great opportunities to build your network of contacts as well.

In addition, contact an HR manager or any manager in the companies of interest for an informational meeting where you can pick their brain. This takes time but be persistent and you may be able to get some managers willing to meet you or at least talk to you over the phone. If you have friends or know people in the company, ask them to refer you to the HR manager or other managers for you to meet. LinkedIn is a good place to locate HR staffing personnel and other recruiters. Explain to them that you are exploring different positions to help you consider the best fit as you start out your career. Also use your network of contacts who work in different jobs and in different organizations.

Although these efforts require a significant amount of time, it's worth the investment. As a new graduate, it's easier to obtain an entry-level position from a list of job openings and in different organizations in a company. Companies are more willing to train new college hires as they will likely start in entry-level positions. On the other hand, if you are an experienced professional in a current job, it's more difficult to move into a different position since the new position will likely require someone with experience.

How to Write a Compelling Resume

A resume enables you to get your foot in the door. While a resume does not get you a job offer by itself, it can get you an interview opportunity that can lead to a job offer. Unless the employer already knows you, a prospective employer will review your resume to determine if they want to interview you. While your ultimate objective is to get a job offer, it's not the goal of a resume. In all my professional years, I very rarely saw or heard of offers being made from just reading a resume, no matter how compelling. The resume's key objective is to generate enough interest for potential employers to want to interview you. You have a much better chance of getting an interview if you produce a compelling resume that matches well with the job's requirements and makes you stand out against other candidates. In this chapter, I'll show you how to write such a resume by focusing on two areas: style and content development. In addition, I'll discuss the type of content to include in your LinkedIn profile.

Write a Compelling Resume

Style

- Maximum 2 pages
- Simple format ready for online submission
- Easy to read and follow
- Bullet-point format
- Come alive with power words
- Attention to detail

Content

- Aim to generate interest for employers
- Create a foundational generic version
- **1. Contact info and job objectives**
- **2. Summary of skills/qualifications**
- **3. Education summary**
- **4. Experience summary**
  - *Include both paid and volunteer experience*
- **5. Relevant hobbies/technical skills**
  - *Enhance your appeal and value-add*

Create a LinkedIn profile

- Platform to stay connected
- Leverage resume content
- Endorsements and recommendations
- Keep profile fresh
- Take it as seriously as resume

CREATING RESUME STYLE

This is about creating the look and feel of your resume, including how to format, how to organize and how to make it easy to read and follow.

- **Keep a resume to maximum two pages**. If you are a new graduate without much work experience, a one-page resume may be sufficient. Focus on quality instead of quantity. The person reviewing your resume could be an HR (Human Resources) staffing recruiter, outside recruiter, or a hiring manager. Due to the sheer volume of resumes to review, I would typically only spend a few minutes on each resume. I would look to see if you meet the required qualifications and how you stand out against other resumes. If your resume is longer than two pages, I probably would scan through your resume even quicker, which increases the likelihood of missing important information you want me to know. Moreover, a long resume indicates a possible lack of discipline to be succinct and lack of ability to prioritize key information about you. A four-page resume listing everything you have done in your career will likely create a negative impression even before the manager begins reading it.

- **Keep the format simple**. Since you will likely submit your resume online, PDF or text format is appropriate. Some employers use programs to scan for certain keywords on your resume to determine your potential

THE RIGHT JOB FOR YOU

fit. Use normal font size for the body content (10–12 point). There's no need to use fancy fonts or colours.

- **Make the resume easy to read and follow**. Use bullet points instead of long sentences. Try to keep each bullet point to one or two lines. If the manager has a few minutes to read your resume, you don't want them to have to re-read over certain things because they weren't clear on what you meant to say. Moreover, using bullet-point format encourages you to be succinct and to the point.

- **Make your resume come alive**. Use active, "power" words as appropriate. For example, use "I led" instead of "I was involved," "I initiated" instead of "I assisted," and "I delivered the project results ahead of schedule" instead of "I was able to finish…"

- **Check for spelling and grammar errors**. Misspelled words or grammatically incorrect sentences can turn a good resume into a mediocre one and could negatively cloud the reviewer's opinion of you. It also indicates laziness and lack of attention to details. So it's worth it to spend a few minutes running your resume through spell and grammar check.

DEVELOPING RESUME CONTENT

The objective of a resume is to generate interest for potential employers to want to interview you. To start off, focus on developing a great foundational resume that highlights your skills, experience, education, qualities and accomplishments without focusing on any specific company. In addition, be creative and use any relevant and factual information that will help you stand out and put you in as good a position as possible. Then as you find a specific job you want to apply for, you can tweak this foundational resume for that job. If you did a good job creating the resume, tweaking it to match the requirements should be quick and without a lot of effort needed.

The general structure of a resume includes:

1. Contact information and job objective

2. Summary of skills/qualifications

3. Education summary

4. Experience summary

5. Relevant hobbies/interests/other technical skills

It's not necessary to include a References section. If the employer wants to check for references, they will ask you at that time. The order between Education Summary and Experience Summary can be interchanged. If you have a fair amount of experience, you may want to order your experience before education.

1. **Contact information should be straightforward.** For your contact information, use a phone number that you can be easily reached at. Usually this is your cell phone.

Don't list a phone you use infrequently. Since managers are usually busy, they would like to be able to talk to a candidate live on the phone when they call. If they need to leave a message, you run the risk of playing phone tag since it's a good possibility they will not be available when you call back. Also use an email account you check regularly. If an employer sends you an email message regarding your job interest and doesn't hear from you in a few days, they'll assume you're not interested.

For job objective, reserve a line to fill in the job title/description when you want to apply for a specific job. For example: "Seeking a challenging and interesting Business Analyst position that will enable me to use my skills and grow with the company (Job Requisition# 123REQ)." Remember to include the job requisition number if there is one so you can ensure the resume will reach the right person.

2. **Summary of Skills/Qualifications**. This is the most important section of the resume. This is where you can summarize a few key points you want the managers to remember about you because they're not going to remember everything on your resume. The analogy here is similar to writing a thesis paper where you put your theme and main points at the beginning of the paper. Instead of having the managers try to come up with what to remember about you, why not make it easy for them by stating it upfront. This section should include a short list of 4–5 skills and accomplishments that best match the position's requirements and put you

in the best possible light. Here are some example bullet points for graduating college students:

▷ Strong technical skills and experience that match very well with the position's requirements

▷ Track record of successfully leading different groups of people on multiple school projects

▷ Exceptional communication skills developed through communication classes and internship at ABC company

▷ University department Dean's List for three consecutive quarters

▷ Demonstrated ability to get up to speed quickly, solve problems and go above and beyond to get things done right and on time

You need to support these skills and qualifications by providing proof in subsequent sections of your resume. If you have difficulty writing this section first, skip it and work on the last three sections. After you have completed those sections, pick out key nuggets and include them in your Summary of Skills/Qualifications section.

3. **Education Summary**. Many graduating students don't make full use of this part of the resume. They simply list their college major and a few classes they completed.

As a result, they miss an opportunity to reveal special accomplishments or unique skills they have learned. It's not enough to just list out your major and classes taken. This does not separate you from others. Focus on pointing out and highlighting any excellent results you achieved with your education. Some specific suggestions:

▷ Include college major(s), degree, high GPA. If you have a minor degree, list it as well.

▷ Include relevant and successfully completed classes as well as results and accomplishments from significant research projects, group projects or other completed papers. Also highlight the skills you developed. For example, learning leadership skills from leading a group project, developing analytical skills from research projects, writing skills from publishing papers, etc.

If part of your education programme involved working with a real company on a specific project where you/your team delivered tangible benefits to the companies and at the same time, learned and developed concrete skills, you should definitely highlight this experience. This is especially useful in situations where a company requires a certain amount of work experience that you don't have. However, this kind of school experience can serve as a good substitute for the lack of real work experience.

In a business class I taught, we had a business plan group project. Students formed in teams of four and their objective was to create a business startup that serves an unmet need in the community. They developed a complete business plan with detailed marketing strategy, operational plan, financial analysis and forecast. Upon completion of the project, each team gave a presentation on their business plan. For a member/leader of the team, this would be a great experience to include in their resume – highlighting skills they developed, including leadership, communication, collaboration, analytical and presentation skills. The hiring manager would view this positively.

▷ Include key awards and accomplishments during your educational years such as Honour Roll, Valedictorian, Dean's List, top 10% of class, scholarships, etc.

4. **Experience Summary**. I want to emphasize two important points here. First, focus on highlighting your positive results and accomplishments on each of your jobs. Many people only provide a list of job responsibilities and activities they performed. While it makes sense to describe the job, it's not enough and is only a small part of what you should include. You want to make yourself stand out as much as possible. Just listing your job responsibilities does nothing to highlight you. Pointing out good results and accomplishments will separate you from others. Secondly, think about your paying as well as non-paying jobs and volunteer work experience.

Work experience is not limited to paid positions only. The experience and skills you gained in your volunteer work are as meaningful and valuable, and in many cases, create a better impression on hiring managers than a paid position.

If you have a long work history, put more focus on recent employment experience (within the last five years). If you limit your resume to two pages, you will not have enough space to cover every job in detail. Here is how to develop the content for the Experience Summary section:

▷ For each position, list the job title, company's name, location and employment duration.

▷ Describe briefly your job and key responsibilities. Keep this to one or two lines.

▷ List successful results and key accomplishments. Think about how your results contributed to your team or your company's success. Excellent results include finishing a project ahead of schedule or below budget, helping sales to exceed target, saving company cost, increasing customer satisfaction, and improving quality of product and services. It's best if you can show quantitative results. For example, finishing a key project two months ahead of schedule or reducing the defective products by 20% is a tangible result. When I was a product manager working on a new computer product, we completed the project three months ahead of schedule. This allowed the company to launch the product in a peak-buying season and as a result, the company gained an advantage in the market. You bet I included this in my resume. One more point: you need be able to support your claims and explain them in detail if you're asked about them in the interview.

▷ Think about examples that demonstrate your value and standing in the company, such as bonus awards, excellent job review/ranking, praise from managers, company recognition, customer/partner appreciation, employee of the month/year award, significant salary raises and stock grants. Don't forget to include anything that makes you look good and separate you from the crowd. This is not the time to be bashful.

▷ Another way to show your skills and qualities is highlighting the times you were a leader or played a leading role in motivating people and driving the team to get the job done. This shows you were a skilled, dedicated leader and not just an average employee. Companies don't want to hire average employees.

5. **Relevant hobbies/interests/technical skills**. Use this section to highlight yourself in other areas you have not covered in the resume. Many people give this section little attention, putting the same hobbies most people

put on their resume, which doesn't convey anything unique about them. Here's what you should do:

▷ Include hobbies or interests that enhance your appeal to the position or provide even more support for the qualities you highlighted. For example, if you are a long-distance runner and have participated in long-distance races, including this hobby demonstrates your self-motivation, dedication and discipline. If you play a musical instrument, including this hobby shows you have creativity. If you participated in competitive events in sports, technology or arts, including this shows your passion, competitiveness and motivation to succeed.

▷ If you hold professional certificates, even ones not related to your area, including them demonstrates your range of interests and curiosity. If you belong to the IEEE association or have a professional accounting certificate, highlight it. Although I was a product manager for a high-tech company, I also had a real estate licence. I included this in my resume to highlight my people skills, negotiation skills and communication skills – all important qualities for my product management job.

▷ Include organizations you belong to and hold a key position in, such as Treasurer, Finance Analyst or Marketing Specialist. All this goes to show your ability or at least, your motivation to develop and improve key skills required in the workplace.

▷ Any other technical skills that highlight you even more, such as expertise in certain technology areas – web design, for example – or deep knowledge about specific and unique accounting audit processes.

CREATING YOUR LINKEDIN PROFILE

LinkedIn is a popular online networking site for professionals. It's a platform where they can stay connected, share information, stay current in their field, research for job opportunities, and advertise themselves. The good news is you can leverage your resume's content for your LinkedIn profile. With LinkedIn, you have an opportunity to personalize your resume and tell more of a story about you. Below are a few things to keep in mind when creating your profile.

• You can expand on your resume's specific content. While I advocate keeping your resume content succinct, you can use your profile space here to add more colour to your bullet points. If you mentioned a great accomplishment in your resume, you can tell a story behind that result. For example, during your internship, you delivered a proposal that impressed company management so much they decided to implement it. On your profile, you can elaborate on what made the proposal compelling and go into more detail about your role and contributions.

- With your LinkedIn profile, you don't need to be as narrowly focused on your professional skills as you are in your resume. You should include other skills and areas of interest and expertise to demonstrate your versatility, curiosity and aspirations.

- Another excellent LinkedIn feature you can use is posting endorsements and recommendations. A powerful way to promote yourself is to have other people endorse you. Solicit your co-workers, managers, professors and others to write you a recommendation on LinkedIn or endorse your specific skills or expertise. It's also a great way to support your claims. For instance, if you claim that you have excellent leadership skills and ability to work with people to get things done, having your manager or colleague's testimony is powerful proof.

- Sharing photos, posting videos or articles is an effective way to stay connected with people as well as highlighting your unique skill or expertise. You can keep your profile fresh by posting professional or personal updates as often as you like. Through LinkedIn, you can greatly expand your network of contacts. It suggests people you have either a direct or indirect connection with to link to your network. Through LinkedIn, I was able to stay connected with people whom I would have otherwise lost touch with years ago.

HOW TO WRITE A COMPELLING RESUME

- Take your profile as seriously as you take your resume. Be thoughtful and careful about what you include in your description. Since anyone can look at your profile, you don't want to post anything that could affect your image negatively or show you in a bad light. This advice applies to your LinkedIn account as well as all your other social media platforms. Employers may check your social media postings, and anything that raises a red flag can potentially hurt your employment chances.

ADDITIONAL TIPS

- Don't include a cover letter unless you are asked to provide one. This is not a common practice. Most managers only have time to read the resume to determine your fit for the position.

- Don't include references on resume. This is not needed. If you get far enough into the hiring process, the employer will ask for references at that time. So use the extra space on your resume to promote yourself.

- Don't use slang, jargon or acronyms that are not easy to understand, unless the acronym is common and widely understood (such as IEEE). If you need to, spell out the acronyms. People whose native language is not English may not understand slang easily.

- Don't include personal information that may negatively affect your chances of getting an interview, particularly if you don't know who will be reviewing your resume and whether that person has any biases. You need to use your judgment here; there is no right or wrong answer. For example, a student asked me whether he should include in the resume his membership in a gun association. Since neither he nor I knew if the potential hiring manager had any strong opposition to people owning guns, I advised him to use his judgment and to think whether this detail was relevant and helpful to the position and whether it was worth taking the risk.

- Don't lie. While you definitely should make yourself look as good as possible, be sure that every fact or claim is accurate and can be supported. In today's world, your records can be easily verified. You probably have heard of famous people losing their jobs because they lied on their resume. On a consulting service project with a high-tech company, the prospective employer did a background check on me before I started the job. When I received the report, it provided a detailed record of the last ten years of my life.

- The use of Artificial Intelligence (AI) scans is a potential approach companies may use for initial sorting and matching. Your resume should focus on relevant key words for AI scanning. Read the job description carefully and leverage your LinkedIn and other social profiles to understand the job position's keywords and to provide an expanded view of your brand.

- Have a look at some good examples of resumes as www.careeratwork.net.

Interview with Confidence

Before interview

- Know the target: Company, job details, interviewers

- Prepare list of potential questions and your answers:
  - Job skills
  - Problem-solving skills
  - Teamwork
  - Communication skills
  - Dedication/commitment

- Prepare questions to ask the interviewers
  - To learn more about the fit with your career goals

During interview

- Make good first impression Punctuality, attire

- Speak clearly

- Maintain eye contact

- Show energy/enthusiasm

- Buy time to respond if need

- Ask leading questions to highlight yourself

- Ask for clarifications

- Turn negative questions to your strengths

- Get contact information

Don't

- Don't ask about salary/benefits during interview

- Don't talk bad about previous company/manager

- Don't take anyone with you for the interview

How to Handle Interviews with Confidence

What is a successful job interview? You may think a successful interview is one that results in a job offer. While that is the desired result, you can have an excellent interview without getting a job offer. That may sound contradictory and illogical, but let me explain. The fact of the matter is you don't have much control over the hiring decision. You don't know how many other people also interviewed for the job or what factors the hiring manager considered in making the decision. You may not receive a job offer even though you felt you did well in the interview. For instance, I have seen one case where there were two qualified candidates, each with different strengths. The manager ended up choosing one person over the other due to experience level. Or in another case where there were three equally qualified candidates, one female and two male candidates, the hiring manager, wanting to have a more diverse team, decided to offer the job to the female candidate.

However, do not despair. In my mind, a successful interview is one where you were prepared, gave your best effort answering questions, engaged the interviewer fully and were satisfied with the information you learned about the company. Your goal for the interview is to do so well you make it easy for the manager to want to hire you. Managers have to juggle many balls at work. When they need to hire a new employee for their team, they have to squeeze the time into their schedule. It takes a lot of time to conduct the hiring process, including writing the job description, completing the required paperwork, posting the job opening, reviewing resumes, interviewing candidates and negotiating the job offer.

Let's take an example. A manager has five candidates going through the in-person interviews and it takes a total of three hours to spend on each candidate. That takes almost two work-days, not including the time the manager has spent reviewing other resumes or the amount of time the interview team spends interviewing. If the manager is really impressed with you and satisfied that you are an excellent fit, they have a great incentive to hire you quickly because that would save a lot of time. It's in your best interest to do your best to make it as easy as possible for the manager to make the hiring decision.

However, even if you did not get the job but did well in the interview and left a good impression, the manager will remember you and would likely recommend you to other managers who have openings. I saw this many times in my career. When I was looking to hire a forecasting specialist, I had two qualified candidates but could only hire one. Even though I did not hire Ted, I kept his resume. When I learned two weeks later that a colleague was looking to hire a demand planner – a different position but with similar skillset requirements – I recommended Ted. After interviewing Ted, the manager offered him the job. This example illustrates the importance of being thoroughly prepared and giving your best effort to impress the hiring manager and interviewers. If you achieve that, be satisfied with your effort, regardless of the outcome.

In this chapter, I will cover two areas: what to do before your interview and how to conduct yourself at the interview. This chapter is especially helpful if you will be interviewing with a multinational company that has employees in other countries with a different culture from that of your country.

BEFORE THE INTERVIEW

How you prepare for an interview is extremely important as it determines how well you will perform at the interview.

- **Know the company**. Inevitably one of the interviewers will ask why you are interested in working for this company. If you are stumped by this question, you just hurt your chances of getting a job offer. After all, why should I hire you if you cannot tell me why you are interested in joining my company? Another key reason to know about the company is for you to determine whether this is a company you want to join. Company information is available publicly. The company website provides most of the relevant information – its products, services, reputation, culture, etc. Other online websites such as Indeed. com or Glassdoor.com also give good insight about the company's culture, reviews from employees, etc. Let's say you find out company ABC is known for offering innovative products, has been growing faster than its competitors and is rated one of the top places to work. When asked, you can tell the interviewer you are impressed with the company's innovative products, its reputation as a great place to work, its leadership in the industry, and you would like to be a part of this growing company. Take a little time to research and learn about the company. It'll be worth your time investment.

- **Know the job details**. Knowing as much about the position as possible will help you prepare for the interview, both in the potential questions you may get as well as the information you want to find out. Before the interview, you should have a copy of the job description describing the main responsibilities, people you will be working with, your role in the overall organization and the job requirements. Usually the job description is listed on the company's website. If you don't have a job description, ask the company representative to email you a copy. Sometimes you can find out useful information by asking the representative for any specific qualities or requirements the hiring manager is especially keen on. Be sure to read the job description carefully to help you anticipate questions about the position and formulate your answers.

- **Know the interviewers**. This is not a must but will help you feel more at ease at the interview. Many companies have a team of people to interview you. These tend to be people you will be working with. Ask for the interview schedule if you did not receive one. It should show each interviewer's name and their title. This reveals their job level status and the function they work in. Today, many professionals are on social media sites, such as LinkedIn, where you can get relevant information on them. Knowing something about the interviewers helps you think about what questions you want to ask them. For example, if a person has been with the company for several years in a few different positions, you can ask this person about the company's support in developing employees and providing different opportunities. At the very least, when you meet with the interviewers face to face, your knowledge about them will put you more at ease and help you establish a rapport with them.

- **Prepare a list of potential questions and your answers**. Different companies may have differences in what they want to find out about you. However, I find that there are some common categories companies want to focus on:

1. Job skills

2. Problem-solving skills and creativity

3. Teamwork – how effective you are working with other people

4. Communication skills – your ability to listen and understand people's viewpoints as well as express your thoughts clearly and compellingly

5. Dedication/commitment – your willingness to take the extra step, to go above and beyond to get the job done

Many companies use a behavioural approach when they interview you. Simply put, instead of asking you if you have the ability to do something, such as: "Are you good at presenting?" the interviewer gives you a specific situation and asks you to respond. This type of open-ended question enables the interviewer to glean greater insight about you because it requires you to think on your feet, consider things thoroughly and give well-thought-out answers. For example: "Give me an example of a situation where you had to present to a large group of unhappy customers and how you managed it." Regardless of how the interviewer asks questions, preparing for the interview as a behavioural interview will help you do your best.

I will describe the five categories above in more detail. For each category, think of a few questions and your own answers to them. Also, for each category, think of a couple of specific examples to strengthen your answers and highlight your qualifications. Why examples? Your examples add "meat to the bones" of your answers, personalize you and make you unique. Before we dive deeper into these areas, take an example of two answers to the question: "Are you a good communicator?"

- Answer 1: "I consider myself a good communicator with good verbal and writing skills. I've always been able to express myself clearly and persuasively."

- Answer 2: "I consider myself an excellent communicator with strong verbal and writing skills. For example, during my previous job at XYZ, I led a major product launch where I developed the marketing materials, provided training to sales people and presented to many customers. I received excellent feedback on my communication skills."

The second answer is by far a better one. The first answer is so general anybody can give the same answer. It does not distinguish you from other candidates. Answer 2 demonstrates your ability with a specific example.

Now let's look at the categories in more detail.

1. **Job skills.** This is simply to find out if you have the technical skills to do the job. If you are applying for a position in the accounting department, you must have good accounting and finance knowledge. The job description I mentioned earlier should list specific job responsibilities and tasks you will be doing as well as the job's requirements. This is a fundamental category. If you cannot demonstrate you have the knowledge and

technical skills to do the job, you won't get the job offer regardless of how well you do in the other categories. The questions here are specific to your field. If you are a software engineer, you may be asked to write a short program using a specific programming language. If you are a finance analyst, you may be asked about cost/benefit analysis. If you apply for a job as a marketing analyst, you may be asked about conducting customer surveys or return-on-investment methodology. Make sure to study the job description because it will give you a good idea on how to prepare and brush up on your technical skills.

2. **Problem-solving skills.** Practically any job will involve business problems and require the ability to solve them. Problems may range from customer issues to sales and quality issues. Demonstrating your ability to solve problems will help you stand out among the candidates. While most people can follow instructions, people who take the initiative to solve problems are viewed as high performers and valuable assets to the company.

The question you got could be a general question such as: "How do you go about solving a problem?" or you could be given a specific problem situation and asked to solve it. For example: "You are working in the customer support department and the customer's level of satisfaction has been declining for the past two quarters. What would you do to improve customer satisfaction?" Many fall into the trap of jumping to solutions. That is a wrong approach. Since you have not worked at the company and don't have much insight, the interviewer doesn't expect you to give specific solutions. Whether it's a generic question or a specific one like this example, the interviewer is looking to understand your approach to problem-solving, your thought process on how you would go about arriving at the answer. A smart approach to solving problem is: (1) understanding the problem; (2) finding out root causes of the problem; (3) brainstorming and identifying possible solutions; (4) weighing the pros/cons and benefits/costs of potential solutions; and (5) deciding the best solution.

For the "customer satisfaction" example above, this is how I would answer the question: "First, I will go about finding out the root causes of the problem by analyzing customer data, customer feedback reports and by talking to customers and salespeople if possible. Once I identify the root causes, I will engage with the appropriate experts inside and outside the company to brainstorm specific ideas to improve customer satisfaction. Then I would analyze the pros/cons and cost/benefit of these ideas to determine the best one for the company and then make the appropriate recommendation." And if you have time, give an example from your previous experience where you solved a problem successfully. This will strengthen your answer even more.

3.**Teamwork.** This is to find out how effective you are at working with people, or more specifically, how you handle difficult situations working with others. For the vast majority of the time at work, you will be working with other people on certain projects. The ability to work well with people to get things done is highly valued, and companies examine this quality closely in deciding which candidate to hire. Questions on teamwork may be phrased like this: "You are a leader working on a project where one of your team members is not meeting his deadline and putting the team's project at risk. How would you handle this situation with this individual?" With this kind of question, avoid jumping to the answer. When I used this question in interviews, I heard candidates say they would try to get the person off the team or fired. While removing the person from the team may ultimately be the answer, it's more important to try to understand why, and then come up with the appropriate plan. After all, it's difficult to address this situation with the team member if you don't you know why he was not meeting his commitment.

Early in my career I faced a similar situation with Joy, a team member. Fortunately, a more seasoned colleague advised me to go talk to her to find out why. Joy told me she had some recent family medical issues that required her to leave work unexpectedly and early sometimes. As a result, she missed a few team meetings and fell behind on her work. Once I heard this, I offered to help take on some of her tasks and she accepted. She was very appreciative and felt bad she hadn't come to me sooner. She was embarrassed about her situation and didn't want to reveal it.

The moral of the story here is that there could be a number of reasons for this situation and it's prudent to find out before taking action. If asked this question, this is how I would answer: "First of all, I would let him know the team depends on him meeting his commitment in order for the project to stay on track. Then I would tell him I'd like to know why so I could find ways to help. Once I know the reasons, he and I can brainstorm potential solutions. If we reach a dead end, I'll escalate to the manager for help and, at the same time, let him know I'm taking this action to ensure that the project stays on track." My answer shows that I am a team player who goes out of my way to work with people to resolve issues and get things done. At the same time, I understand the team goal and, if I need to, I would escalate to make sure the project stays on schedule. While the team member may not like my escalation, he would respect me for being straight with him. This also enables me to build trust with him for any future project we may work on together.

4. **Communication skills.** This is to probe your ability to listen and express your views clearly and persuasively. Regardless of what the job is, you will likely be working with other people, people from your team, from other functions in the company as well as outside the company. The ability to communicate effectively is critical to your success and that of the company. You will be tested for this skill in the interview. Think of a couple of examples from your experience where you used your communication skills successfully to persuade a

colleague or manager to go with your view, or where you gave a strong presentation to a new audience. The interviewers will judge your ability in this area by watching to see how you come across and listening to your answers. A lot of this is about your style – do you come across confident, persuasive and engaging? Here are some questions you may get:

▷ Your manager gives you an additional project and you feel that your plate is already full. How do you handle this situation and how do you say no?

▷ How do you rate your communication skills? Which part of your communication skills needs to be improved the most?

▷ Describe a situation where you had to give an important presentation to a new audience and how you handled it.

▷ The company creates a new exciting project that many people, you included, want to lead. I am in charge of selecting a project manager for this new project. Convince me you are the best person to lead this project.

5.**Dedication/commitment**. We want to know about your work ethics and your commitment to get the job done. Think of a time when you took the extra steps and went above and beyond the call of duty to help out co-workers to ensure the team project was completed successfully and on time. Also think of an example where you identified a need that was not being addressed and took the initiative to work on it. This shows you have the company's best interest in mind and you are a team player willing to do what it takes to help the team succeed. Possible questions you may get include:

▷ Give me an example when the project you were working on with other people was at risk of missing an important deadline, and describe what you did to get the project back on track and completed on schedule.

▷ Give me an example where you show initiative to take on a task important to the company even though it was outside your job scope.

▷ You have a situation where your manager asks you to work the next weekend in order to meet a project deadline but you already had other personal plans. Describe how you would handle it.

• **Prepare a list of questions you want to ask the interviewers.** Think of the interview as a conversation. Although most of the time you will be answering questions, you will have time to ask questions. It's an opportunity to find out information you want to know about the company, about the job, about people you will be working with. This helps you determine whether this is the right company and the right job for you. Since time is limited, be selective about which questions you want to ask. Here are some potential questions:

- ▷ What would be my specific duties in the first 90 days? (This is a specific question for the hiring manager.)

- ▷ What are the key success factors in this job?

- ▷ What are the key challenges in this job?

- ▷ What are the key characteristics of successful people at this company?

- ▷ What experience and growth opportunities will I be able to gain from this job?

- ▷ What do you like about the company and what are the challenges you see for the company in future?

- ▷ What are the next steps in the hiring process? (This is a specific question for the hiring manager.)

AT THE INTERVIEW

You have done your homework in preparing for the interview. Now you are at the interview with the opportunity to show how qualified you are and why the company should hire you. To accomplish this, you need to know how to conduct yourself.

The key word here is "how". A lot of it is about optics – your personality and the way you carry yourself. In all likelihood, the interviewers don't know you and they're meeting you for the first time. Therefore, the impression they form of you will be what they remember. Following these guidelines below will help you perform your best and help you come across as confident, energetic and engaging.

- **Speak clearly**. If you have a soft voice, this is an area you need to pay attention to. If the interviewer has to strain to hear you or have to constantly ask you to repeat, it doesn't make for a good conversation and it brings into question your ability to communicate. Also, when we are nervous, we tend to speak faster than usual. If you need to improve in this area, practise and focus on speaking clearly and loudly enough for the person sitting across the table from you to hear comfortably.

- **Maintain eye contact**. It's a good way to establish rapport and to show you are engaged in the conversation. Imagine what impression you would create if you were looking at your feet while answering questions. You give the impression of being disengaged, timid and not confident.

- **Show energy and enthusiasm**. When I have other people interview my candidates, their initial feedback on the candidate oftentimes is about their energy level – whether the candidate had good energy, showed enthusiasm and was excited to be there. If you maintain eye contact and engage in the conversation, your energy will show. You don't have to jump up and down to show your enthusiasm

On one occasion when I was interviewing a candidate, Kelly, for a position on my team over lunch, I asked her when she would like to start. I expected a typical answer of two weeks after offer acceptance. Instead, she answered: "How about after lunch?" I knew Kelly was joking and it made me laugh, but her answer showed her energy and excitement about joining my company.

- **Buy time when you need to**. When you get a question you're not sure how to answer, don't get rattled or feel you have to give an answer immediately. You can buy some time to think about it and come back to answer later in the interview. You can buy time by saying: "That's a good question. Let me give it some thought and get back to you in a little bit if that's okay?" Then while you're answering other questions or talking about other topics, you can think about it in the back of your mind and when ready, re-engage the interviewer on the question.

- **Ask for clarification**. If you get a question you're not quite clear on, don't hesitate to ask for clarification. It's important that you understand the question clearly so you can answer appropriately. The interviewer would be happy to elaborate on the question and this may also give you some clues on what the interviewer is looking for. You can say something like: "I just want to make sure I understand your question, would you mind repeating it for me?" or "I want to make sure I understand, you're asking ABC. Is my understanding correct?" After giving your answer, you can also ask a follow-up question to determine if you were on the right track, such as: "Did I address your question?" or "Is there anything else you would like me to cover?"

- **Turn negative/tough questions to your strengths**. You may get questions such as: "Tell me about your biggest weakness" or "Tell me a major mistake you made." The weakness question is intended to understand if you are objective in your assessment of yourself and what you are doing to address it. Don't answer: "I have no weaknesses." You come across as arrogant and not having self-awareness. The way to answer this question is to give a weakness trait that shows your desire and effort to mitigate it, and at the same time, can be seen as having upsides. One such trait is impatience. If you are a "go-getter" type of person who drives to get things done right and as soon as possible, you tend to have less patience with other people. However, you recognize that other people may work at a different pace and you are consciously working to give them more space and assistance to get their work done. Moreover, impatience also reflects positively on your motivation, dedication and commitment to complete the job. The mistake question is intended to determine what you learned from your mistake and what you have done differently going forward. Think of a work mistake you made that you learned from and worked to rectify.

- **Get contact information**. Thank the interviewers and ask for their email address at the end of interview. This helps in case you have a question you want to ask but didn't have a chance during the interview. You may run out of time before you get a chance to ask your question. This also is a good way to build your network of contacts.

ADDITIONAL TIPS

- Show up five minutes early. Don't be late. Remember what I said earlier about making a good impression. Also bring a copy of your resume and a pen to take notes.

- Dress business professional unless you are told otherwise. If you're not sure, ask your contact if the company has a preferred dress code.

- Turn your phone off or put it on silent mode. You want to eliminate any potential distraction during your interview.

- Take notes as needed. This helps you to ask follow-up questions and may give you additional clues on what the interviewer is looking for from their questions.

- Don't ask about salary, vacation days or benefits during the interview. When you get a job offer, you will know what the offer includes and you will have an opportunity to negotiate the terms of the offer. You have limited time in the interview so ask questions that are most relevant and helpful to you. In addition, you want to avoid giving the impression that you care most about the money and benefits.

- Never talk bad about your current/previous company or your manager, whether they deserve it or not. It may create a suspicion in the interviewer's mind about your professionalism.

- Don't get rattled by the question. Think about the category of the question being asked and refer to your mental list of answers and examples. Also remember that you can always buy time.

- If you have an interviewer who is not disciplined and rambles on instead of interviewing you, don't be confused or think you don't need to say much. If the interviewer finishes the interview without knowing much about your qualifications, it's a lost opportunity. Find opportunities to ask questions that will help you talk about your qualifications. You can accomplish this by asking, for example, about the qualities that will enable you to be successful. By listening to the interviewer's answer, you can then highlight your own qualities with relevant examples. Or you can ask for the challenges they see with this position and prepare to respond appropriately.

- Be aware of posting things on social media sites. Don't post things that may reflect negatively on you. I have seen examples of people not getting a job offer because of comments or things they posted on their social media page. On one occasion, I interviewed a candidate for a management position on my manager's team. She was very qualified and seemed a good fit for the company. As part of the background check, my manager learned of insulting remarks on her Facebook page about a previous manager. This raised a red flag to my manager and made him reconsider his decision.

- Attend the interview alone and don't take anyone with you to the reception area or worse, to the interview room. You may find this suggestion unnecessary and amusing, but it has happened. You want to come across as independent and a self-starter who doesn't need hand-holding.

- Last but most important, practise your interview and role-playing with a friend or someone you're comfortable with. This will give you the confidence when you're at the real interview.

HOW TO HANDLE INTERVIEWS WITH CONFIDENCE

TIPS FOR PHONE AND VIDEO INTERVIEWS

In addition to the discussion above, there are a few specific things to keep in mind when doing your interview over the phone or video call.

- Have the information you want with you to refer to, such as your examples and answers. However, do not read from them. It's easy to notice if someone is reading instead of talking. Have the materials there as references, but talk normally on the phone.

- Your voice is the main instrument to show your energy and engagement level. It's even more important to make sure the interviewer can hear and understand you clearly. So be sure to speak clearly and loudly enough. Don't mumble or whisper. Think of the interview as two-way conversation. Engage the interviewer by asking clarifying questions, asking about the job, and giving examples in your answers.

- If English is not your native language, make sure to speak clearly and don't mumble. If your accent is a bit heavy, you may need to speak slower. Pause from time to time to confirm that the interviewers understand what you said by asking them if they have any questions or want you to explain something in more detail.

- Some companies use a different interview format to screen candidates. For example, instead of interviewing over the phone or video, the interview is conducted online without a live interviewer. You may be videotaped for this session. Through an online website, you are given a series of questions, one at a time, to answer verbally. After reviewing your recorded interview, the company representative or the hiring manager will decide whether to invite you in for an in-person interview. With this interview format, you need to be even more thorough in your preparation since you cannot ask for clarification or buy time to think about the answers. Even though it may seem awkward talking to a computer screen, you need to make sure you stay engaged as if you were talking to a live person. Smile, stay relaxed and keep your eyes on the screen as you answer the questions. If you're look-ing down or away, the reviewer would see your head instead of your face.

· Video-conferencing interviews are getting more popular. It's time-efficient for the hiring companies. Preparing your appearance and readiness over the computer screen is important. Pay attention to your video camera angle, background and lighting. For multinational and international companies, keep in mind the time difference in your scheduled interview.

As an interviewer, I am particularly impressed with candidates who come in prepared and ready for a meaningful discussion. Asking questions is key in showing your strengths, your interest level and to end the interview session on a high note.

HOW TO HANDLE INTERVIEWS WITH CONFIDENCE

Since there is typically a pool of candidates, we have to pick the best candidates. Aim to be unique and different while being true to yourself so you can stand out. There is no advantage if you are seen as average in the pool of candidates. I often suggest to people I mentor to think about what personal brand and related attributes they want to establish.

POTENTIAL INTERVIEW QUESTIONS

1. You are given a business problem. Our sales this quarter were below target. What steps would you take to increase sales?

2. What accomplishments are you most proud of?

3. What are your biggest strengths? Biggest weaknesses?

4. Tell me about a major mistake you made.

5. How do you resolve a conflict with a co-worker at work?

6. If you're working on a team and the project's going to be late because a member of the team is not meeting his commitment, what would you do?

7. Your manager gives you an additional project and your plate is already full. You can't take on any more responsibility without jeopardizing your work. How would you handle this situation?

8. What did you like and dislike about your last job? And why?

9. What classes did you like/dislike in school? And why?

10. What drives you? What motivates you? How do we help you do your best work?

11. Where do you see yourself three years from now?

12. Describe a difficult challenge you faced and how you handled it.

13. Describe a situation where you had to give an important presentation to a new group of audience and how you handled it.

14. The company has created a new exciting and popular project. I am in charge of selecting a project manager for this new project. Convince me you are the best person to lead this project.

15. Why are you interested in joining this company?

16. If you had a chance for a do-over, what would that be and why?

17. Tell me a time when you were under a lot of pressure to meet a tight deadline and how you handled it.

18. What did you like and dislike about your last manager?

19. Tell me a time you had to multi-task and how you prioritized and handled the tasks.

Negotiate a Job Offer

Should you negotiate
- If you have multiple offers
- 10% higher starting pay is equivalent to 2–3 years of increments

How to negotiate
- Understand the parameters
- Assess possible trade-offs
- Determine desired outcome and walkway value
- Estimate company's acceptable limits
- Counter-offer options

What to negotiate

MONETARY
- Starting base salary
- Relocation expenses
- Temporary housing
- Stock options
- Restricted stock units

NON-MONETARY
- Work schedule flexibility
- Job responsibilities
- Travel requirements

Tips
- Don't come across arrogant
- Don't issue ultimatums
- Don't be confrontational
- No "fake news"
- Be professional and positive
- Don't burn bridges

How to Negotiate a Job Offer

This chapter focuses on multinational companies whose headquarters are based in the United States or in other Western countries. Other companies may have some differences in their hiring process. However, they're likely to include many elements of the hiring procedure and process described here.

One common question graduating students ask me is if they should negotiate when they get a job offer and if yes, how to do it. My answer is you should absolutely negotiate, especially if you have multiple offers. The best time to negotiate for the best compensation package, of which salary is a big component, is when you receive the job offer because that is when you have the most leverage. By making you an offer, the employer showed that they wanted you more than the other candidates. They would not want to lose you over the compensation package terms and they will more likely do what they can to get you to say yes.

While salary is the most significant variable, there are several other components to a job offer. A job offer includes salary as well as other incentives such as stock options and a sign-on bonus. With respect to salary, each job position is associated with a job level and each job level has a predetermined range of salary from which the HR manager and hiring manager can decide on the amount to offer. The salary offered would likely be somewhere in the middle or in the lower half of the range. This leaves room for negotiation if necessary and for future salary increases for the employee. If they offer you a salary near the top end of the range, the manager has limited flexibility on how much salary raise he can give you in the future. The company also has guidelines on the flexibility of the other benefits, such as how much cash to offer for sign-on bonus.

The Human Resource manager would likely be the person you negotiate with since HR has the final approval on many of the offer terms. The HR manager consults with the hiring manager and makes counter-offers based on the hiring manager's input. However, there may be other components that make sense for the hiring manager to negotiate with you directly.

Companies may differ on the degree of flexibility of the offer components. Some companies are firm on salary but flexible on stock options or sign-on bonus. Do your best to find out where they are limited and where they have the flexibility. Here are some of the typical job offer components:

MONETARY COMPONENTS

The HR manager plays a major role here in helping the hiring manager.

- Base salary.

- Stock options. These are shares given to you that you can exercise over a number of years at a given price. For example, 5,000 shares at $30 per share price vested over four years. If you sell all 5,000 shares after four years at $40 a share, you gain $50,000 pre-tax.

- Restricted stock units. These are shares given to you outright ($0 cost) vested over a number of years.

- One-time sign-on bonus. Typically 1–3 months of the base salary.

- Relocation expenses. This covers your moving expenses if you have to relocate from another city or state.

- Temporary housing. This covers you for a temporary period while you try to find permanent living arrangements.

Let me explain the importance of the starting salary. Companies determine employee salary raises and bonuses as a percentage of the employee's base salary. For example, if your starting salary is $70,000 a year and you get a 5% raise and 10% bonus after one year, you receive a $3,500 raise and $7,000 cash bonus. On the other hand, if your starting salary is $80,000 and you get the same 5% raise and 10% bonus, you receive $4,000 raise and $8,000 cash bonus. Comparing the two scenarios, you receive $1,500 more with the higher starting salary. Assuming you stay in this job for 3 years and get the same 5% raise and 10% bonus every year, you will earn a total of $4,500 more. So if you were able to negotiate for a higher starting salary, you not only get paid more in your base salary but also more in raises and bonuses.

One more point. Typical salary increases are small because they're based on the overall company's performance, projected budget and the entire employee population. Typically, an average salary increase is in the range of 2–5%, not very much. Because of this, negotiate for the best salary you can in the beginning.

NON-MONETARY COMPONENTS

The hiring manager is likely the decision-maker on these items and the person you would talk to directly.

- Work flexibility. For example, how often you can work at home.

- Job responsibilities. In addition to your core job responsibilities, are there other exciting and interesting projects you can be a part of? Can you get assigned to a company-wide project where you get more exposure to other aspects of the company? Is it possible to work on a temporary project in another country, if that's what you like?

- Vacation benefits. If you move to this company after a long period of employment with a previous company, you probably have less vacation days. You can negotiate to get more vacation days than the company policy allows. However, this tends to be a handshake agreement between you and the hiring manager and not something that would be in writing. The downside is, if your manager leaves the company, you may lose this benefit. Also note that many companies now have the "unlimited vacation" policy. There is no set amount of vacation days for employees and approval for taking vacation is between the manager and the employees. Obviously, for these companies, vacation benefits are not a negotiating term.

- Travel flexibility and requirements. Do you want to travel more or less? If you prefer to travel less than what the job stipulates, you may be able to negotiate for less business travel or travel to business locations closer to home. Before you consider negotiating on this term, make sure you are clear on the importance of business travel in your job. If this is a critical part of the job, it may not be an option for you to negotiate.

CASE STUDY EXAMPLE

Let's examine and negotiate a job offer scenario.

- You are a new college graduate and recently received an employment offer as a Business Analyst from an HR manager of Stay InTouch Inc., a social networking company.

- The manager expressed in the offer letter that the company is very excited to have you join its family. The company's offer includes $70,000 a year in base salary and 2,000 shares of stock option.

- You will need to relocate to another state to join this company.

- The offer seems low to you.

- The job market is good for new college graduates this year based on credible market information. However, you don't know for sure but guess that the company has other candidates in the pipeline.

- You currently don't have other offers, but you had excellent interviews with two other companies and received positive feedback.

- You want to negotiate a better job offer.

HOW I WOULD NEGOTIATE THIS OFFER

Let's look at the approach I would take:

1. Understand the true issues and parameters of the negotiation.

2. Assess where possible tradeoffs exist.

3. Determine your desired outcome and the walkaway value.

4. Make your best estimate of the other side's walkaway value.

I'll use these steps to help me with my approach:

1. Understand the true issues and parameters of the negotiation. I am negotiating the job offer as a package, not just the salary, although it is a big factor. While only salary and stock options were listed in the offer, I want to think about other components that are important to me. I am currently tight on money; I would need it for my move and to find temporary living arrangements when I start my job. In addition, I'm interested in international experience and I want to explore the possibility of working overseas on an interesting project.

2. Assess where possible tradeoffs exist. From my thinking in #1, the variables I want to negotiate on are, in order of importance: salary, relocation expenses, sign-on bonus, stock options and opportunity to work on a temporary assignment overseas. Therefore, I want to negotiate for a higher salary and relocation expenses/ sign-on bonus in exchange for receiving a smaller number of stock options. Working overseas is a bonus and I can ask for it if I cannot get an agreement on other components.

3. Determine your desired outcome and the walkaway value. Before I do this, I need to find out as much

information as I can from the company and research thoroughly about the job market. Specifically, I need to talk to the HR manager to find out how flexible they are on the offer terms and whether they are open to other items not mentioned in the offer letter. To do this, I need to ask a lot of questions:

- "I'm very interested in joining Stay InTouch and I'm doing my due diligence to gather as much information as I can to help me with my decision, and given my understanding of the job market, the salary offered seems low. Do you have any flexibility on the salary figure?"

- "Can you let me know where the company is more flexible and where it's not?"

- "Are there other items not included in the offer the company would be open to discuss?" Be prepared to give your own suggestions if asked.

- If the manager does not bring up the items you have in mind, ask: "Does the company have the flexibility to provide relocation expenses and a sign-on bonus?"

- I generally find employers are willing to share information with you because they want you to join them and would try to make it work for you. I would also talk to the hiring manager and ask about the flexibility on the work items that I wanted. Let's assume that I found out the company has a little bit of room to increase the salary, no flexibility on the stock options, and is willing to offer relocation expenses and sign-on bonus. Typically, the hiring manager owns the budget for some of these expenses and he has to decide how much he can afford to spend on me. In talking to the hiring manager, I also found out that he's open to a temporary overseas assignment in the second year, depending on my job performance.

With my knowledge about of the company's flexibility and my own assessment that I may get at least one more offer from another company, I come up with my desired and walkaway value. My walkway value is: 5% above the offered salary, 2,000 stock shares and $5,000 relocation expenses. My high value is: 20% above offered salary, 2,000 stock shares, $5,000 relocation expenses, and 2 months of salary for sign-on bonus. I want to shoot for achieving the final agreement somewhere in this range. However, because I like the company a lot, I would accept an offer closer to my walkaway value if that is the best I can get. I also understand that I'm willing to turn down the offer if I don't achieve at least the walkaway value because I feel confident I can get a better offer from another company.

4. Make your best estimate of the other side's walkaway value. Based on the information I have, my best guess of the company's lowest acceptable value is somewhat

higher than my lowest acceptable value, but since I'm not absolutely certain, I am comfortable keeping my current walkaway value.

The final step is to make a couple of counter-offers that are attractive to me. By offering multiple offers, I encourage the HR manager to consider which one of the counter-offers is best for the company. This is better than offering only one counter-offer which the HR manager has to either accept or reject or come up with another offer that may not be ideal to me.

ADDITIONAL TIPS

- Don't be arrogant or give the impression of arrogance. Coming across as a hotshot and having an "I don't need this company" attitude is a real turnoff. Even if you end up joining the company, you're not starting off with the best impression.

- Don't give ultimatums. "Take it or leave it" or strong-arm tactics usually don't work. There is no need to do this, especially since you don't know for sure where the company is flexible or firm. If your "take it or leave it" offer doesn't work for the company, the negotiation is over. Keep in mind no one is irreplaceable in the company, not even the CEO, and you're not a must-hire. Companies almost always have other candidates to choose from. If you do decide to use this tactic, be sure you're ready to walk away. But my recommendation is to stay away from this tactic.

- Don't be confrontational or adversarial. Keep in mind this is one of the companies you want to join and they also want you since they have made you an offer. Maintain your professionalism and cordial discussions in your negotiation. Don't push them into a corner, use unprofessional language or an accusatory tone if you don't like the offer terms or feel the company is not accommodating. Even if the company plays hardball, stay calm and don't let your emotions get in the way. After all, this is a business negotiation.

- Don't lie. Don't make up stories or offers you don't have in order to gain leverage. The business community can be a small world where people know each other, and if you're caught lying, the company may rescind the offer and you have a black mark on your reputation.

- Don't push past the limit and try to go for every last dime you can get. If you have an offer that's in the range between your high and lowest acceptable value, consider taking it and not pushing it further. You need to use your judgment here. If you and the company have gone back and forth a few times and it feels like they're running out of patience, it may be a good idea to accept. Keep in mind the adage "Penny wise, pound foolish". It's more important to start off on the right foot with a good impression than to get a little more money and leave a bad perception.

- Be professional in your communications with the company. When in doubt, ask for clarification. Maintain a positive attitude and show the company representatives that you very much are interested in joining the company. Even if things do not work out or you decide to take another offer, explain to them honestly and professionally. If you have conducted your negotiation in good faith, the company representatives would understand if you have a better offer they could not match. Keep in mind to never burn bridges because you never know if you will cross paths again with them.

- There are good websites offering useful information about specific companies. For example, in the US, Glassdoor.com site provides information on a specific company's annual salaries by job titles, feedback on the management team, etc. Check for similar websites for companies in the region you're applying in.

How to Start Your Job on the Right Foot

The initial weeks when you start your job provide you a good opportunity to take advantage of the "honeymoon" period to learn the lay of the land, to get up to speed and make a good first impression. Given the pace of work these days, new employees have less time to learn the ropes and are expected to contribute quickly. Employees who prove to be quick learners and contributors will make a great impression, gain credibility and confidence with co-workers and management. You need to have a plan to hit the deck running on the first day and this chapter will show you how. Your company may have some differences from the information presented in this chapter, but the bulk of information from this chapter should be useful to you.

How to Start on the Right Foot

BEFORE DAY 1

1 Get ready for Day 1
- Get assigned a buddy
- Connect early for IT access needs

2 Read up on corporate info, plans

3 Settle living arrangements (if relocating)

STARTING YOUR JOB

4 Create company ecosystem map

5 Meet your buddy and get oriented

6 Get connected to IT system

7 Understand from your manager
- Understand how to work with them

8 Get introduced to key work counterparts
- One-on-ones to build rapport

9 Company product/service training
- Great platform to connect with others in the company too

10 Attend team and company meetings
- Shadow your manager to observe
- Great insiders' view

11 Familiarise with work tools/systems

12 Start off with regular hours
- Staying a little late could help
- Starting late/leaving early gives bad impression

13 Familiarise with corporate "look and feel"
- Presentation format
- Content and style guidelines

HOW TO START YOUR JOB ON THE RIGHT FOOT

WHAT TO DO BEFORE YOU START YOUR FIRST DAY

Before your start date, there are a number of tasks you can do to put yourself in a position to be productive from day one on your job.

- Work with your new manager to make sure all your IT equipment and services will be in working order and ready for you to use on the first day. Submit all your IT needs soon after you accept the offer to give the IT department time to order equipment and set up. A few days before you start your job, follow up to make sure things are on track and in case of any issues, you have time to resolve them before your first day. Don't just trust that everything will be there in working order the day you start. Your manager may forget to follow up due to his busy schedule and he would appreciate a reminder from you. Moreover, ask your manager for a buddy – someone with a good reputation at work and is valued by the manager. This person is a valuable resource for you to learn the ropes from. Ask the manager to set up a one-on-one meeting with your buddy on your first day.

- Obtain approval and permission to access company services you need for your job. Your manager can help you with this and get the approvals needed. Double-check with your manager and don't assume it will be taken care of. For example, meetings conducted over video or audio conference are quite common. If you schedule these meetings, you need to have the system access code to use the equipment, or if you will need to access and use company sensitive data, you need to receive permission and the passcode since accessibility is restricted to certain employees. It's frustrating and a waste of time when you start your job and have to wait a few days to be able to access the data.

· Familiarize yourself with company materials. Ask for company materials relevant to your job that you can read before you start. This may be your manager's annual team plan, status reports on current activities or projects, product or project plans, last quarter's CEO presentation, etc. Reading these ahead of time will give you a feel for the current state of the company business and insight about your job. Your manager should be aware of company policy on confidential materials to determine which documents you can have access to.

· Get settled in if you are relocating. When moving to a new town or city, you will need to take care of your living arrangements and other personal tasks. Try completing them before you start your job so you don't have to spend time and energy trying to settle in and do work at the same time. These tasks can consume a lot of time and if you have to take time out of work to finish, that will slow you down at work. When you start, you want to focus your energy and time to get up to speed as quickly as possible.

HOW TO START YOUR JOB ON THE RIGHT FOOT

WHAT TO DO WHEN YOU START YOUR JOB

Use your first couple of weeks to get a good feel for the lay of the land as it relates to your job. Understand the ecosystem in the company – how things get done, how people work and communicate, important processes, key people you will be working with, decision-makers and influencers, and how decisions are made. In addition, spend time obtaining knowledge and insight on company products and services. Having a good understanding of the company's ecosystem is paramount to your job's success.

Think of this ecosystem as the Global Positioning System (GPS) of a new city you just moved to. This smart system shows you the different routes to get from place A to place B, with all the variables that can affect which route you're going to take, including speed limits, traffic flows and road closures. Moreover, these variables can change at any moment, depending on the time of day, weather conditions and traffic flow changes. The smart GPS helps you determine the best route to take and navigate through these unpredictable obstacles. Without knowledge of your company's ecosystem, it would be similar to driving without a GPS in trying to get to your destination and not having a clue how to get there.

- Create the ecosystem map. With help from your buddy and manager, start putting together an ecosystem map pertinent to you and your job. This is a chart of important people whom you will be working with, key influencers, decision-makers and potential executives who could be your champions. This group

105

includes people in your organization as well as other functions. Make notes of their title, organization, job responsibilities, keys to working with them, and if possible, their reputation in the company. Then get to know them because your success depends on how effectively you work with them and help them be successful in their job. A second key part of the ecosystem is to capture how things are done in the company – decision-making processes, communication methods, operational processes, project management, teamwork dynamics and unwritten rules. Your buddy and manager are great resources for this.

- Meet with your buddy and spend a good amount of time with this person on the first day. Ask them to share with you how things get done, how people work and communicate, key people you will be working with, how decisions are made, and who the influencers, decision-makers and potential advocates are. Use the information to help complete your ecosystem map. Find out the best ways to do things at work, major issues and "elephants in the room" you should be aware of. In addition, get your buddy's thoughts on your manager – the best ways to work with your manager, his hot buttons and his strengths and weaknesses. Also ask your buddy to show you how to access and use the company IT system, and take you on a tour of all the facilities so you can be familiar with the buildings and the people working in them.

- Use your computer and IT systems to go through the login process to make sure the systems are in working order and you have access to the services you need. If you run into any issues, call the helpdesk. You should also get into the company's internal website and familiarize yourself with the company's services, including Human Resources, market research and IT support. In addition, through the company internal website, you can learn about other organizations and their role in the company.

- Meet with your manager. Find out his or her expectations, how best to work together, hot buttons, how your manager wants to be updated, and the key challenges and priorities. Also ask the manager similar questions as what you asked your buddy, especially the important co-workers and managers you need to be on the good side of, as well as people who can be your advocates. If time permits, discuss with your manager about your annual plan. Otherwise, schedule a meeting for this. Typically, every company requires the manager to have a yearly plan for each employee. This plan is critical to your performance review and it includes the objectives, expected results and timelines.

- If you are working remotely and will not have regular face-to-face interactions with your manager, make sure you and your manager work out a way to stay connected and keep you in the loop. The most common feedback I hear is that remote employees feel disconnected from the rest of the company, don't know what's going on and don't receive real-time information. Since you and your manager will not be able to touch base frequently, commit to having regular one-on-one meetings. Moreover, discuss how to keep you in the loop. Some managers are not on the ball when it comes to sharing information, especially sending a message out to their team. It's not top of mind and they tend to share information verbally and often, informally. This doesn't work for you. I would suggest using a portion of your weekly one-on-one meetings for your manager to update you. In addition, find out if your manager uses or would consider using a trusted onsite employee to help disseminate information to the rest of the team, especially remote employees.

- Schedule one-on-one meetings with the key people you will be working with, including the project lead, team members and other managers. Try to meet with them in the first two weeks. Your goal is to get to know them, find out their needs, expectations, priorities, issues and concerns, and how you can best work with them. If possible, meet with them over lunch where they'll have more time to talk with you. Finally, since it's not feasible to meet everyone, send out a greeting email to introduce yourself. If you work with other people in remote locations such as another country, set up a phone meeting where you can introduce yourself.

HOW TO START YOUR JOB ON THE RIGHT FOOT

- If your company offers product and/or service training classes, take them as soon as you can. Other types of classes may also be available, including meeting facilitation, public speaking, project management and time management. This is the time to take advantage of these classes. You get the knowledge you need and gain the confidence to do your job. In addition, attend the company orientation and meetings set up for new employees with company executives. This is an opportunity to hear directly their thoughts and ask them questions.

- Attend team and other company meetings to get a feel for how the company works, key issues, challenges and decision-making process. The people you work with will let you know what meetings you should attend. Ask your buddy and manager for suggestions on meetings that you can tag along to observe even though you're not required to be there. In addition, find out about customer visits and briefing events where customers meet and talk with company representatives about a variety of topics. Contact the company speakers for approval to come and observe. Even if your job doesn't require you to interact with customers directly, this is a good way to learn about company information being shared with customers, their issues and needs, and observe how the company representatives interact with them.

- If there are data mining and analytics programs you need for your job, learn and practise using them during this time. Moreover, if there are external services available to the company from industry service firms, request access to these services if they are relevant to your job. These services include industry reports, research projects and consultation.

· Keep your regular work hours when you start your job, or better yet, stay a little later at work. Since you probably have a lot to learn, it's a good idea to use the extra time to get up to speed. Coming in late or leaving early leaves a bad impression.

· Familiarize yourself with the company "look and feel" guidelines for creating media and other materials. For example, when you create presentation slides for a meeting with company suppliers, you need to use the company's content and style guidelines. It helps you present a consistent company image and saves you the headache of hearing from the company's brand police.

For those who like a head-start, some of the above can be done offline before your first day. From outside resources in the public domain, you can get some understanding of the company's strategy and direction. While it may seem foreign, it will form the foundations for you to connect the dots when you are in the system. That will give you an accelerated head-start, especially if you are amongst a large group of new employees. You need to breakout from the pack as early as you can.

You should not expect to stay only in one department or function for your entire career and expect regular job progression and promotions. In some companies I was involved with, cross-team experience is a promotion criterion and hence, job rotations and career developments are required. So take full advantage of the initial period to understand the breath of the company. Familiarity with the broader company culture helps lay a strong and wide foundation for your career. HR is a great resource for you to reach out to in these areas. Refer to the "How to Work with Human Resources (HR)" chapter for more details.

From my personal experience, my move into marketing function was one of the best things that happened for my career. Despite the early reluctance, it was like a fish taking to water. I wish I had pursued that change much earlier. So, my advice is to start early in your career to keep an open eye, be curious and to explore interesting, even out-of-the-box opportunities.

Different Types of Managers

Bully manager

- Lowers your morale
- Impacts self-confidence
- Could damage your career and life quality

Handling unfair treatment

- Keep it professional, not personal
- Document paper trail
- Start with annual plan – deliverables and timelines
- Know how to utilize HR
- Copy HR and next-level boss
- Negotiate: exit/stay/move to another team

Difficult managers

Give proactive frequent updates

- Hands-on/micromanager
- Clueless manager
- Absent manager
- "Go where the wind blows" manager
- "I'm smartest" manager
- Disorganised manager

Develop self-help options

Work successfully with your manager

- Adapt to your manager's style
- Be low-maintenance
- Make manager's life easier
- No surprises
- Complement manager's weaknesses
- Approach with solutions

How to Work with Different Types of Managers

In the 25-plus years of my professional career, I have had 15 managers, the shortest stint being three months and the longest four years. They all had different managing styles and personalities. This averages about one manager for every two years. There were a multitude of reasons for having gone through this many managers: changes in my job, my manager's job or the company organization. Some management changes were my choice while others were not. In talking to other professionals, I found my career situation was quite similar to theirs, and I suspect yours will not be too different. It's not unusual to have many different managers in your career. While your career may not have the same frequency of management turnovers, don't be surprised if you have a new one every couple of years. If someone tells you that only you can control your career success, it's only half the truth. In addition to your talent, effort and hard work, situational dynamics and upper-level managers are important factors as well. While this seems unfair, the fact is life can be unfair. Your managers are an important factor to your career's exposure, opportunities and growth. Learning to embrace and work with this reality is as important as doing your work.

You seldom get to pick your manager. Of the 15 managers I had, there were only two that I knew and wanted to work for. Accept the fact that throughout your career, you likely will work for many managers with different management styles; therefore, to be successful in your career, you need to know how to earn their trust and work with them effectively. In this chapter, I'll share the best practices to work with managers in general, regardless of their specific management style. Then I'll cover specific types of managers and how best to work with them.

BEST PRACTICES TO WORK SUCCESSFULLY WITH YOUR MANAGER

- **Adapt to your manager's management style**.
  Many problems occur between employees and managers as a result of miscommunication or misunderstanding. Your initial meetings with your manager are good opportunities to figure out how to work effectively with him. Ask your manager about his managing style, "hot buttons", expectations and how he likes to work with his employees. Find out if he prefers to communicate via email or face to face, how frequently he likes to have one-on-one meetings with you, how often he wants to be updated on your work, what kind of information he cares about and how other successful employees have worked with him. Having this meeting to hear straight from the horse's

mouth will save you headaches and frustration later on. Once you have a good idea of his management style, write down what you have learned and store it somewhere you can easily refer to later.

- **Low maintenance**. Because managers need to do their own individual work as well as manage a team of employees, they're quite busy. Just attending all the required meetings as part of their management responsibilities consumes a significant amount of time. As a result, managers love low-maintenance employees – employees who don't require a lot of time from their manager, are not frequent complainers and don't need a lot of hand-holding to do their job. This, however, doesn't necessarily mean that a high-maintenance employee is a low-performer or that a low-maintenance employee is a high-performer. I have had employees who delivered good results but were frequent complainers and needed a lot of TLC (tender loving care). These employees can drain a manager mentally and soak up his energy. If you are self-motivated, can stay focused regardless of distractions, and work independently when given direction, guidance and support from your manager, he would appreciate you immensely.

- **No surprises**. This is one of the biggest pet peeves managers have. They don't like to be caught off-guard, especially with bad news. If your manager's boss asks him about some bad news that he wasn't aware of, he comes off as not being on top of things and looks bad. This is not going to make your manager happy. Tell him. If your project is running into a major problem, risking delays and you're unsure of what to do next, let your manager know and ask for help sooner rather than later. Resist the urge to solve it yourself. You may feel you are failing if you can't find a way to solve it on your own; however, that is what a manager is for. Chances are he has been through these experiences and can help you. It's better to escalate to him now than for him to find out through his peers, or worse, his manager. In addition, keep your manager in the loop on important matters. If you're asked to meet with his boss or with other executives and you're not sure if he was also invited, let him know about the meeting, unless you were asked to keep it confidential.

- **Make your manager look good**. Making yourself successful and stand out at work also helps your manager look good. A manager, to a great extent, is a reflection of his team. If the team is doing well and getting the recognition from other managers and executives, the manager looks good and gets the credit as well. If you and your team receive recognition for a job well done and your manager played a role in helping you, thank him. Show your appreciation for his support and make sure his boss is aware of it. Moreover, avoid undermining your manager or throwing him under the bus. When you and your manager are in a meeting with other managers and executives, try not to contradict him directly. Before the meeting, you and your manager should spend a few minutes to make sure both of you know the purpose of the meeting and are in agreement on potential issues. If you hear your manager make wrong statements, determine if you can wait to correct him after the meeting to avoid making him look bad in front of people. However, if you believe you must correct him, do it diplomatically. Don't say: "You are wrong. That information is not correct." Instead, try something like: "I'm not sure if you have the most updated information, let me double-check on that for you." This gives the manager a way out by deflecting the incorrect information off of him.

- **Don't come to your manager with just the problem**. While there can be exceptions, don't come to your manager with just the problem, but come with possible solutions as well. Or at least be prepared to discuss potential options. When you have a business problem you need to bounce off your manager, you can help make the meeting more productive by discussing the problem and then presenting potential solutions you have in mind. This gives your manager options to think through and give his opinions. Furthermore, it shows your proactive effort in addressing the problem and trying to come up with solutions. Good managers know to not give their employees answers but help them get to the answer on their own. If you're about to discuss with your manager a business proposal but you're not sure about your recommendation, share with him the potential ideas you're considering and ask for feedback to help you form a solid recommendation.

- **Make your manager's work life easier**. Managers have a lot of things going on and would appreciate your effort to use their time wisely. There are ways you can help them. For example, when you have a one-on-one meeting, optimize the time with him by being prepared. Before the meeting, send him an email asking for anything specific he would like to cover in the meeting as well as prepare a list of topics you want to discuss. If there are any decisions or follow-up actions, send him a short summary message afterward to ensure that both of you are on the same page. When it comes to performance review, do your homework to prepare him as best as possible to give you a fair review.

  If he is a visual person and understands better with graphs instead of numbers, show him your analysis in graphical form. If there are meetings you can attend without needing him there, let him know and then give him an update afterward. Your manager would appreciate the extra time to do his work. For meetings you need him to attend with you, make sure you spend a little time with him beforehand to brief him on the topic, objectives and any requests you have for him. This will help prevent confusion or miscommunication between you during the meeting. If he doesn't have time prior to the meeting, see if you can walk with him to the meeting and use that time to brief him. My manager and I used this practice quite a bit in my previous job and it worked out well for both of us.

- **Complement your manager's weaknesses**. All of us have weaknesses and managers are no different. Some managers are not well organized, some are not analytical, some are not skilful at creating compelling presentation slides, some are not good at handling details, some are good at managing up but not their employees, etc. If you can discover your manager's weaknesses and even better, if you have skills to complement them, you will become valuable to your manager. For example, if you sense your manager is not good at organizing and managing the details of his department meeting, offer to help with organizing the meeting, creating the agenda, taking notes and keeping track of action items discussed in the meeting. A tactful question such as "I notice you have a lot of things going on, would you like me to organize our staff meetings and manage the meeting agenda going forward?" offers him a solution to consider without admitting his weakness. One of my former managers, a Vice President, was a straight-shooter. He spoke to company executives the same way he did to his employees, without trying to be diplomatic. In a work environment, this sometimes created ill-will even though it was not his intention. One of my roles was to be a sounding board for him in these situations.

You can also be a good partner who watches out for your managers and helps them out of unpleasant situations. I recalled an incident where a team member of mine, Dae Hwan, helped me defuse a situation. In a tense moment of business review cycles, tempers flared and voices were raised. Dae Hwan initiated a sideline call with me. He then advised me to play the good cop and let my other team members to do the tough challenging. It was great advice from him. By watching out for your manager and serving as sounding board, you are not only helping the team, but also helping your boss. It will go a long way to earn their trust. Dae Hwan and I remain great friends and business buddies.

HOW TO WORK WITH DIFFICULT MANAGERS

My focus here is to describe the different behaviours of managers and offer suggestions on how to work with them. It's not my attempt to try to understand or explain their behaviour.

- **Hands-on/Micromanager**. This is one of the more common management types. Throughout your career, you either have experienced or will have the unfortunate experience of working for a micromanager. This manager is a control freak who looks over your shoulder and wants to know everything you're doing, who needs to review your detailed work and often tells you how to do your job. This manager seems to have difficulty figuring out what he needs to know or focus on, so instead, he tries to know everything. First-time

managers managing a team of employees, who were
their peers, often exhibit this type of behaviour. As
they gain more experience and grow into their management role, they may change or moderate their
management style; at least we hope, so for the sake
of their employees. This type of manager may seem to
contradict my contention that managers are busy and
don't have time to delve into their employees' detailed
work. However, this type of manager cannot seem to
help it, even if they're overwhelmed.

Although it's easy to feel frustrated and not empow-
ered, the way to work with a hands-on manager is not
to fight him since it will create a lot of tension for both
of you. Instead, take a proactive approach. In your
initial meetings with your manager, discuss the best
way to work with him. Here you may learn more about
his hot buttons and come to an agreement on working together. He may not reveal his micromanagement
style, but at least you are encouraging him to communicate how he would like to work together. At least he
knows that you're being proactive and that you want
to work with him and not against him. In the initial
period, update him on your work regularly (daily, if you
need to), via email or face to face, whichever works
best. Instead of resisting him, ask him for his opinion
and be open to his comments. Once he feels comfortable that you are open and proactively working with
him instead of keeping things close to the vest, he
will start trusting you more, easing up and giving you
more space. Also by overwhelming him with updates,

he will likely reach a point where he needs to back off, physically and mentally.

Due to an organization change, I once moved to a team with a hands-on manager. Neither of us knew each other much. Initially, she was critical of my work, didn't seem to trust me and wanted me to update her with every single detail. I had always wanted to work independently and felt that I did my best work without the pressure of someone constantly looking over my shoulder. Following the advice of a co-worker who had successfully dealt with this manager before, I made a conscious effort to meet with my new manager frequently, several times a week, to explain my work and ask her for feedback. This routine went on for a few weeks and as she started to feel more comfortable and gained more trust in me, she eased up. Although she was never fully hands-off, we eventually achieved a balance in our working relationship.

- **Clueless manager**. This manager is all talk and little action, all style and little substance. He talks a good game and speaks management speak, but there is no real substance in his words. He doesn't seem to have the skills to run the business and doesn't possess the judgment required to make good decisions. This kind of hiring could be a result of a manager getting promoted into a new function even though he had little knowledge of the new organization. Or he was brought in from another company without much knowledge or experience in the new company or industry. I have seen this happen multiple times in my career. Sometimes an executive wanted to bring in his buddy to run a department, regardless of the person's background or experience. When I was a member of the product marketing team, the GM of our business unit brought in an engineering manager to run our team when our previous manager left the company, even though she had no marketing skills or experience.

Moreover, there are different types of clueless managers. One type is a "Clueless but Harmless" manager who knows he lacks the business experience; so he leans on a few strong people on his staff to help him run the organization. The other type is the "Clueless and Dangerous" manager who does not seem to be aware of his lack of business skills and experience, and often makes decisions on the fly, sometimes depending on whom he heard from last.

At one company I worked in previously, I was Chief of Staff for a Senior VP in the Product Group. He was initially hired to run the engineering department and when his boss suddenly left the company, he was named the acting head. Three months later, his boss appointed him to be the permanent head of the Product Group. Coming from another company in a different industry, his background was in engineering and manufacturing and he had little industry knowledge or business experience. Yet, from day one, he expressed a lot of arbitrary opinions about the business and made rash, ill-informed decisions. He came across as forceful, and people were too timid to push back. He disregarded recommendations from people who had extensive knowledge of the business and, instead, reacted and made decisions based on the crisis of the moment. Because of the lack of experience and judgment, he changed his mind frequently when things did not turn out right, but he continued to make bad calls that cost the company millions of dollars. On top of that, he also had selective memory and was good at deflecting blame onto others. I witnessed this first-hand for almost a year. Whether he realized it or not, he was in over his head and made bad and costly decisions for the company. After three years, when the company reorganized, he was finally reassigned to do "special projects". To me, it was three years too late.

How should you handle this type of manager? Since he craves public attention and has a big ego, try to work with him behind the scenes and persuade him to change his mind and adopt your well-thought-out ideas as his own. Don't contradict or undermine him in public and do your best to not get on his bad side. With the example above, I made the mistake of correcting the Senior VP a couple of times in his meetings and that didn't sit well with him. In my career, I unfortunately have seen some of these managers stick around for years because they were very good at playing politics. My advice is to be patient and find better opportunities outside of his control. But remember to leave amicably and not to burn any bridges.

- **Absent manager**. This is the opposite of the micro-manager. For many different reasons, this manager is not very engaged with you or the team and does not seem interested in your job details or the team's. As long as things are going smoothly and there is no major crisis, he's happy not getting involved in your job. You don't have much interaction with him, other than the infrequent one-on-one meetings or when a crisis occurs. I have observed some managers who fit this category over the course of my career – some became jaded in their job, some reached a dead end in their career and were lost, some were too busy to be involved or, worst of all, some used their position's status to pursue other self-interest goals.

I remember one specific example where a manager moved from another function to manage the team I was on. She had no marketing knowledge, no experi-ence running a product management team, and from the beginning, she did not seem interested to learn. It didn't take long for the team members to see that she was only interested in looking out for #1 – to manage up and make herself look as good and as visible to the General Manager as possible. She latched onto and took the lead on a PR (Public Relations) initiative aimed at promoting the company's leadership position in the industry, and by extension, making the company exec-utives look good as well as getting her name out. She hired a PR consulting firm and spent her time working with them, the GM and his staff. It was crystal-clear she was only using this campaign as a stepping-stone for her career. Her team operated mainly on its own as she spent little time with them. Fortunately, we were senior product marketing people with a lot of experience and didn't need much help from her. If we were a less experienced team, we would've been in a real tough situation.

However, the danger for you with these managers is that they won't care much about promoting their teams or helping to remove obstacles for their employees. In addition, they may not have much influence over their peers, which obviously can affect your success and standing in the company, especially when it comes time for employee reviews or promotions. The downside for the team and me was that she didn't represent us well in the performance ranking meetings because she knew very little about our work, and as a result, we felt we didn't get ranked fairly.

If you have this manager, look for a better situation to move to because this manager will most likely be of no help to you. Meanwhile, you should take control of your own career and do your best to stand out and promote yourself. You can't rely on this kind of manager to look out for you. If you are new in your career and need your manager's support or guidance, my suggestion is to seek out a highly regarded mentor with knowledge of your job functions and lean on this person for guidance and support. Meanwhile, make sure your work is visible to your manager and her boss by updating them regularly on the progress and results of your work. Look for opportunities to meet and present to your manager's boss.

- **"Go where the wind blows" manager**. This type of manager goes with the crowd and has no strong ideas or convictions on how to make decisions or how he wants to operate his organization. He is easily influenced by "key" people outside of his organization and often acts according to whom he last spoke to or who was in his ear the loudest. This manager does not appear to be very self-confident and comes across as paranoid, even emotional at times. The difference between this manager and the "Clueless and Dangerous" manager is this type of manager realizes what he doesn't know and is reluctant to make decisions whereas the latter has no qualms about making decisions, even though they often are ill-informed.

  When I was in the marketing organization, I had a manager who fit this type to a T. She would question what I did, get emotionally upset at me and accuse me of hurting the organization. When I was putting together a budget, I requested two million dollars for a product promotion programme in important international countries. When I met with her to go over the budget, she got upset without waiting for me to explain the rationale, and accused me of wasting company money. She then flatly rejected my budget proposal without further discussion. I was perplexed since this was the normal budgetary practice and was disappointed she didn't give me a chance to explain.

Since I had had extensive discussion with the countries' managers to get their ideas for my promotional programme, I sent her a voicemail message suggesting she touch base with the country marketing managers who wanted to know why they weren't getting the funding they needed. A few days later, she approved my budget for the marketing programme. It turned out she spoke with the country managers and heard their opinions loud and clear.

A good practice in handling this kind of manager is, first of all, to remain calm in the heat of the moment and act professionally. Resist the urge to get personal or emotional. Secondly, this manager tends to be highly influenced by other stakeholders in the company. If some of these stakeholders are involved in your project, get them to be your advocates by soliciting their input and support for your ideas. When you go over your work with your manager, make sure to describe your involvement with the key stakeholders and ask your manager to touch base with them.

- **"I'm the smartest person in the room" manager.** This manager tends to be strong-minded, not easily persuaded and can appear intimidating, especially if he truly is smart. However, this style does not promote individual creativity and limits employee empowerment since they will just default to do whatever this manager thinks is best. I have seen instances where a Senior VP got into a deep discussion on data details with someone in the meeting in order to show he knew more than the employee, even though the analysis was not a significant part of the meeting agenda. His behaviour made the employee feel undermined and belittled, and did nothing to help the progress of the meeting.

If you face a manager like this, you need to realize there is no benefit to getting into an argument to prove who was right and wrong. It can only create ill-will for you if you make him look bad; it's a no-win situation for you. Again, act professionally and let him have his way in the meeting. Take the high road. You don't have to agree with him, just acknowledge his assessment and move on. You can try something like: "Thank you for your comments. I'll check my analysis and get back to you later." Then verify your work and meet with him later to clarify. It could be that you missed something too. If you have a chance to go over your work with him before the meeting, take advantage of it because it's much better to resolve issues one-on-one than in a public setting. Make sure your work is solid so that he would have a difficult time poking holes in it. Moreover, avoid getting into a discussion about details. Rather, focus on your assumptions where you and other people can have a more productive and meaningful discussion. Another good practice is to persuade the manager to adopt your idea as his, which will make him look good while knowing you deserve the credit.

- **Disorganized manager**. This manager is not detail-oriented and not very organized in his own work, not to mention being organized with your work or his team's work. He tends to be forgetful, lose things or have a hard time locating important materials. Don't assume he has the information you gave him or remembers what you two discussed and decided previously. This is not helpful to you or your team, for example, when he has to meet with his boss to discuss the team's work progress.

The way to manage this situation is to pretend that you are your own manager and you organize and maintain the records, documents and materials in a way that you can easily forward to him when he needs them. Take the employee ranking review for example. To help your manager prepare, gather all the pertinent information and materials. Then write a one-page summary of the key results, accomplishments, and people's feedback and any other pertinent information. Put them all in one electronic folder. When you sit down with your manager prior to the performance review meeting he'll have with other managers, use this folder to review with him.

When you meet with him in your one-on-one meetings, find out what major meetings or reviews he has coming up and what he needs to prepare for. Then offer to help him organize the information and materials he needs for these meetings. Disorganized managers tend to realize this is a weakness and would appreciate your help.

HOW TO DEAL WITH A BULLY MANAGER

You believe you have been doing your best, delivering results and meeting goals expected of you; however, you feel you are being treated unfairly by your manager. This manager seems to want to make your life miserable, want to get rid of you or make you into a "whipping boy" for whatever reasons. You don't have to put up with it. I fortunately have never experienced this in my career but have had several colleagues who came to me with this situation. They were miserable, their self-confidence was shot and morale was very low. It's an unproductive situation for both the company and the employee. A good manager should not mistreat his employees and should not get into this kind of situation. Whatever the core of the problem is, it should be addressed and resolved professionally. I don't attempt to know why managers exhibit such behaviour. However, I can suggest ways for you to deal with your manager.

One day I received a phone call from a former colleague, Kim. I knew her well as a professional and as a person. She sounded distraught when she told me how miserable she was in her new job of six months. When she interviewed for the position, the hiring manager told Kim she created this new position with a specific set of responsibilities. She received the job offer and transferred from her current department to the new organization within the same company. But shortly after starting her new job, Kim was told by her manager to stop working on those responsibilities and instead, to take on a new set of responsibilities that she didn't interview for, didn't have experience and hadn't been trained to do. When her manager told her about the new responsibilities, she did not provide Kim a new plan with clear goals, expectations and timelines. Kim asked for training but didn't get it. Then her manager began to demean her, criticize her work harshly in front of her peers and exclude her from the team and other company meetings, even the ones she was asked to attend by people who set up those meetings.

Up until then, she had received excellent reviews and compliments for her work from internal company partners – sales people and international field partners. She had been a high-performer; during her years at her previous organization, she was highly regarded and received a top employee ranking.

Then one day, Kim's manager called her into her office and told Kim she would place her on the Performance Improvement Plan (PIP). When a manager puts someone on PIP, it's usually a step before removing that employee from the company. Imagine the shock Kim must have felt. Here is someone who had been an excellent performer in the company and was now told that if she did not show expected improvement in 30 days, she would be fired. I knew Kim as a high-energy, driven, self-confident person but at that moment on the phone, she was a different person – depressed, hurt and confused.

Before I describe how to go about handling this situation, I want to emphasize one point. Before you conclude that your manager has been treating you unfairly and harshly, you must be completely honest and objective with yourself. You need to ask yourself questions such as: Have I been performing my job according to expectations and goals set out in my annual plan? Have I received at least satisfactory performance evaluation? If there were changes to my responsibilities, were they documented and updated clearly in my plan and did I agree and understand them? Have I received negative feedback since my last review about any issues regarding my job performance? And have I received warnings from my manager about my job performance and behaviour? The answers to these questions will help you make an objective assessment. If you have received good performance reviews and no indication or warning about performance issues from your manager, then you have a strong case.

Let's talk about how to handle this kind of unfair treatment from your manager. Let me tell you a secret about managers. They don't want to deal with employee headaches. More specifically, you can make your manager's life as miserable as they make yours. Managers are typically busy and stressed in their own work life with pressure from their boss, company executives, their colleagues and their employees. They don't want to spend all their time on paperwork and dealing with personnel issues. As an employee, there are ways to make your manager's life miserable. This is not revenge or payback, but a way to keep them honest and force them to do their job properly. However, when you get into this situation, try your best to reach a satisfactory resolution in the end.

- **Keep it professional, not personal**. Even if your manager is petty, condescending and behaves unprofessionally, you should maintain your professionalism. As difficult as it may seem, treat this as a business issue. After all, why waste your effort on someone who treats you like this? They are not worth spending an ounce of your valuable energy on. Don't burn any bridges with anyone, including HR personnel, co-workers or even your manager. This is a small world and you never know whom you will cross paths with in the future. I also view it as a generous gesture on your part to give your manager the benefit of the doubt that they will eventually recognize their mistake and change for the better.

- **Document everything**. You need to keep all the evidence and have everything in writing so you don't get into a "she said, he said" situation that is extremely hard to prove. This includes email messages. When you meet and discuss with your manager, write down the minutes, what was decided or not and next steps. Also keep a record of all materials, especially ones that support your performance and put you in a good light, such as thank-you notes, complimentary messages from people you work with, as well as the accomplishments you achieved – high employee ranking, employee award, recognition and performance review.

- **Start with your annual plan.** Managers are required to have an annual performance plan for each of their employees. The plan describes clear responsibilities, expected results, metrics and timeline for each of the key responsibilities. However, many managers do a cursory job of this just to have it on file with HR and to check off a box on the management list. If the plan is unclear with no specific deliverables and timelines, you can hold their feet to the fire and have great leverage. After all, managers would be hard-pressed to justify their actions toward you when they were unclear to you about your job and their expectations of you.

- **Know how to utilize HR**. Keep in mind that in a dispute between an employee and the company/manager, HR works to protect the company and is not there to help you build a case against your manager or the company. They are there to see if they can make the situation go away quietly. However, they are bound by law and company policies with regard to employment practices. Therefore, keep in mind what I mentioned earlier about the annual plan and having everything documented. In a conflict or dispute, HR's role is to work with the manager to resolve the situation. Moreover, companies typically want to avoid lawsuits, which are costly and can generate negative publicity. You should use HR as a third-party "witness", as someone who has visibility of all the communications between you and your manager, and as someone you can negotiate a solution to resolve the issue.

- **Copy HR and your manager's boss in your correspondence with your manager**. Managers don't want headaches from their employees. Your manager's boss definitely would not want to get involved with this headache either. Similarly, your manager would not want to look bad or have to explain to his boss about the "messy" situation. In addition to copying your manager's boss in correspondence between you and your manager, be sure to copy your HR representative as well as a high-level HR manager – Senior Director or VP level. This is for your protection since you don't know what your manager is communicating to HR about your situation. By copying your correspondences and showing proofs of your job performance, you give HR visibility of your side. HR is required to keep all records of the dispute.

Regarding Kim's situation, I suggested she follow the above steps. Kim told me her manager did not reply to the messages she had sent previously. She then decided to follow my advice to copy her manager's boss. When Kim sent her manager a message describing the lack of a clear plan with no training provided and copied HR and her manager's boss, she received a reply from her manager within one hour. Her manager responded with a much more professional tone. After that, she copied them on everything. Her manager finally got the message that Kim was no pushover and she could make her life miserable as well. Her manager did an about-face and was more cooperative in working to resolve the situation.

- **Negotiate a best deal for you**. By and large, HR wants your manager to resolve the situation with you amicably, and if you are in the right and have leverage, you should negotiate a deal that is best for you but try to achieve a win-win agreement. If you decide you want to leave the company, negotiate a severance package that will also allow you time to look for another job while still being employed by the company. The terms of the package should include payment for a number of months (1–3), length of time to exercise your stock options if you have them, and medical benefits. Each company has different policies on severance packages and you need to get as much information as you can so you can negotiate effectively. If you want to stay in your current job or move to another job in the company, think about the type of job and responsibilities that fit your skills and interests. If you want to stay on the current team, think carefully about your working relationship with the manager and whether it can be repaired.

Kim's story had a happy ending. She decided to leave the company while working through the resolution with HR and her manager. They gave her time to search for her next job and she ended up getting a great job with a successful and up-and-coming company. As a bonus, she was also able to obtain a severance package. Most importantly, she got her confidence, self-esteem and self-worth back.

While companies may have somewhat different personnel procedures and operate a little differently, the approach described in this chapter should help you navigate a difficult situation in your company. However, to give yourself the best possible outcome, you need to understand your company's HR procedure clearly and more importantly, understand how HR and management handle employee-versus-manager conflict. One way to understand is to talk to employees who have been through a management conflict situation. Another way is if you have a friend or know someone you can trust who is in a management role, ask them for advice and insight on how management works with HR.

How to Work with Human Resources (HR)

Human Resources (HR) plays an important role in the company. HR advises the company management team how to strategically manage people as assets and resources. Among key HR functions are design and managing recruiting/hiring, training/ development, salary administration, mediating employee conflicts, etc. In addition, from my management experience, HR also has an objective to protect the company and management team. If there is a dispute between an employee and a manager, don't depend on HR to play a neutral role or be on the employee's side. In these situations, HR is there to keep the company and manager from taking the wrong or potentially illegal actions, not to help the employee win their case. Realizing this helps you know how to work with HR and not get frustrated from unrealistic expectations of your HR personnel. In this chapter, I will describe the roles of HR and how you can utilize HR services.

Work with HR

When to engage

- Need information/clarification, e.g. on job or company policies
- Career counselling/advice
- Negotiate company offer
- Encountered issues:
  - Harassment/abuse
  - Medical treatment program
  - Dispute/conflict
  - Ethical

Understand HR's role

- Serves company's interest, *not* employee advocate
- Supports, advises manager
- Recruitment/hiring
- Benefits/compensation
- Learning and development
- Implements organizational changes
- Facilitates performance review
- Career counselling

What not to expect

- Be your advocate against manager
- Answer to all your questions
- Advocate of change in company
- Honour your sensitive info
- Make decisions for you as employee

How to work with HR

- Proactively engage and learn about their roles and services
- Align with HR/company priorities
- Prepare your facts

HR'S ROLES

Here's a sample list:

- Manages the recruiting and hiring process. HR plays an important role in helping managers hire employees – recruiting, screening, interviewing, putting together offer packages and negotiating employment offers with potential employees.

- Recommends, designs and implements employee benefit programmes, salary and compensation structures for company employees.

- Recommends, designs and implements training and development programmes for employees.

- Implements and manages company organizational changes such as layoffs and acquisitions.

- Mediates employee conflicts and facilitates performance reviews.

- Provides support and tools to managers and employees.

- Provides career counselling to employees.

- Serves company business interest. HR's loyalty is to the company, not to the employees. HR is not there to be an employee advocate. They will do what is in the best interest of the company.

- Serves a support and advisory role to the management team.

WHEN TO ENGAGE HR

In general, HR is a great place to go to for information and clarifications of company policies and programmes – questions such as how to get information, what options are available from company programmes, clarification on particular company policies, etc. This kind of information or clarification is clear and unambiguous. You probably can find most of the information on the company website. If you can't find it, contact HR for answers. Below are some specific items you can go to HR for:

- When you need information regarding your employment, such as your job scope, available training classes and personal leave policy.

- You are a manager and you need to fill a job opening, understand the performance review process or training programmes for managers.

- If you face harassment or abuse at work.

- If you have medical-related issues and want to know what treatment and programmes are available to you.

- When you want career counselling and advice.

- When you want to negotiate the job offer you receive.

- When you have a dispute or conflict at work.

- When you face an ethical issue and want clarification.

WHAT NOT TO EXPECT FROM HR

In general, you should not rely on HR on matters requiring them to give judgment, make decisions or take sides. You should not expect HR to be your advocate when it comes to disputes between you and the company. Here are some situations that show what HR can and cannot do.

- If you bring a dispute between you and your manager to HR, don't expect HR to be your advocate. Many employees don't understand that HR's priority and loyalty lies with the company. Instead, they expect HR to support and fight for them when they escalate a work-related issue with their management. Unfortunately, they end up walking away disappointed. Primarily, HR is there to listen and to keep management out of trouble.

- If you face harassment or abuse at work, by colleagues or managers, you need to escalate this to HR. They take this situation very seriously. Companies care greatly about public perception and don't want to be sued. Moreover, companies don't want to have the perception with their employees that they let these situations fester, and they don't want to risk causing morale issues in the workplace. HR will take action because it is in the company's best interest to have this addressed and resolved as quickly as possible.

- Don't expect HR to provide you answers to all your questions, especially if the information is sensitive or confidential. HR knows much of the company's sensitive information but is not allowed to reveal it to you. For example, if there's an impending change to the company organization, HR personnel would know this well in advance since they have to manage potential changes to employees' reporting structure, relocation and employment status.

- Don't expect HR to be a leader or a change agent in the company. They are there to primarily support company management. It is more of an exception when HR plays a lead role in making breakthroughs in the workplace. A common complaint many employees have had for years is the forced ranking distribution that managers have to adhere to. This type of ranking system creates unhealthy competition among employees and results in low morale in the workplace. This has been in place for decades, and only in recent years have companies started to change to a less restrictive evaluation process.

- HR doesn't necessarily need to honour the confidential or sensitive information you share with them. In some instances, HR is required to share the information with company management such as knowledge of employee harassment or illegal actions. If you want to share with HR in confidence, disclose the nature of your topic and confirm with them whether this will be kept confidential.

HOW TO WORK WITH HR

If you know how to work with HR effectively, they can be a good partner and good resource. Here are some suggestions.

- Understand what services HR provides. When you first join the company, take a little time to learn about their services and support resources, tools you can use, different processes to follow, etc. Many companies have an internal website where you can find all or most of this out. You should also meet with your HR representative to introduce yourself and learn about their role and effective ways you can work with them.

- Have facts and information in writing when you meet with HR, especially on a controversial issue. Typically you will meet with an HR representative and the person you have the dispute with. View the HR representative as a third-party witness you want there to have and record the information you present. Make sure you can support your position with facts. I had a colleague who felt that her manager was undermining her work and reneging on an agreement to have her work on a certain highly visible project. She requested a meeting with HR and her manager. Since she did not have the proof to support her claim, it became a "she said, he said" situation. She didn't accomplish much in that meeting. After that, she learned to document decisions, agreements and next steps in her meetings with the manager as well as writing down specific instances where her manager undermined her. Because the last escalation was not successful, he was overconfident and did not change his behaviour. A few months later my colleague escalated again to HR, except this time, she was prepared and able to back up her complaint. HR had no choice but get her manager's boss involved and he was reprimanded. He eventually left the company.

Rely on HR as a resource to support you, to provide suggestions, counselling and guidance, but don't rely on them to make decisions for you or to be your advocate in potential disputes between you and the company.

In China, those born after 1990 are known as *jiulinghou* – the post-1990s generation. I asked these young employees in China on what help they needed most when they first joined a new company. Top of mind is to better understand the company culture and how to blend in. HR is a great place to start for this. While we can learn a lot from our managers, HR has a more company-wide picture. For a newcomer, reaching out proactively to the HR team would add another source of information and networking, and very importantly, make a good impression as a keen learner.

"I'm not concerned that I am not known,
I seek to be worthy to be known."
— Confucius

As a business leader, it's always at the back of my mind to work closely with HR in spotting talent. In this VUCA (volatile, uncertain, complex and ambiguous) world, potential is seen as more important that current capabilities. Early-career employees should value interactions with HR as exposures to talent scouting. According to my HR partners, they first look for motivation. Motivation is a stable factor and often comes across subtly. Also, potential could be the "engine" that propels top talent to perform. Therefore, we must look inside us to unlock the motivating factors. That will not only help us invest our energy in things that matter, but also help the HR community recognize the talent potential in us.

The other potential talent indicators often mentioned in talent conversations include curiosity, insight, engagement and determination (*21st-Century Talent Spotting*, Claudio Fernandez-Araoz). Once again, HR is a key partner here and can play a key role in helping you bring out these desirable qualities.

How to Ask for a Raise

Understand increment factors
- Salary structure
- Performance review
- Promotion
  - *For larger jump in pay*

Reasons to justify
- Pay under minimum wage
- Uncompetitive pay vs peer companies — *Not eas[y]*
- Uncompetitive pay vs peer employee
- Performance review done "unfairly"

Approach (good negotiator)
- Understand the issues and parameters
- Establish desired outcome and walkaway value
- Estimate acceptable range
- Explain information to gain manager support
- Listen for manager's response and options
- Gain clear "next step" and timeline
  - *Minimum to highlight concerns and gain extra attention*

Tips
- Prepare with research from web resources
- Personal hardship not a reason to justify
- No "entitlement" mindset
- Avoid ultimatums or threats
- No lies!
- Don't over-push the line

How to Ask for a Raise

Before we discuss the question of how to ask for a raise, it's important to understand the salary structure and the impact that performance review has on salary increase. In this chapter, we will cover how performance evaluation impacts salary review as well as examining reasons that may merit a raise and an approach you can use when you meet with your manager.

In a typical salary structure of a company, each job is associated with a job level that is tied to a salary range, i.e. the salary of all employees with that job level falls in that range. Different job levels have different salary ranges and the higher the job level, the higher the salary range. When you're hired, your salary is likely to be in your job level's salary range. As long as you are in the same job level, your salary increase cannot push your base salary above the upper limit. If you're near the upper limit, in order to increase your pay significantly, you need to be promoted to the next job level.

UNDERSTANDING HOW PERFORMANCE REVIEW IMPACTS SALARY INCREASE

Formal job performance and salary review is usually done once a year and changes in salary are based on how the employee is evaluated. Many companies still use the forced distribution ranking system where employees are ranked relative to their peers, while other companies evaluate employees individually instead of relative to their peers. Regardless of evaluation method, you are evaluated on two dimensions: (1) the results you produced versus expectations; and (2) your effectiveness in delivering the results. The outcome of your performance review plays a key role in how much salary increase you'll get.

HR provides guidance for managers to manage the salary increase they give to their employees based on their evaluation. The salary increase guidance can be changed year to year, depending on a number of factors, including company business results, market condition and competitive environment. Another thing to be aware of is that your manager has a fixed budget to administer the salary for all his employees. He has to decide how to allocate salary increases so as not to exceed his budget limit. While this is not your concern, it's good to be aware of the constraint your manager faces.

The amount of your salary increase is determined by two factors: the outcome of your performance review, and where your current salary is in your job level's salary range. I think employees put too much emphasis on salary increase. Generally, the salary increase is not significant. If you are ranked in the middle of the pack or you delivered results that met expectations, you may get a 2–3% raise, nothing to write home about. If you are ranked in the top 25% or you delivered results that exceeded expectations, you may get a ~5% raise – a little more but not a huge increase by any means. For example, if your salary is $80,000, a 5% raise comes out to $333 more per month pre-tax and deductions. It's an okay raise but nothing too exciting. The way to significantly increase your salary is to get promoted to the next job level, where it's not uncommon to see a 10% salary increase.

POSSIBLE REASONS TO JUSTIFY A RAISE

Before you sit down and request your manager for a raise, you need to be self-aware and objective about the reasons to justify a raise. "I am not able to keep up with my bills so I need to get paid more," "My friends are getting paid more than I am" and "I haven't gotten a raise in a while" are not relevant reasons to justify a salary increase. Achieving a high ranking or an excellent performance review is the best way to get a raise. Do your best to maximize your chances of getting an excellent review. Before you approach your manager, examine closely the possible rationales to support your request for a raise. Here are the possible reasons:

- You are underpaid for your job level in the company. One way to determine if your salary is within the salary range of your job level is to ask your HR or your manager for this information. The company should have a salary table showing the salary range for each job level by job function in the company. Although it's not common, I have seen cases where an employee's salary was below the minimum range of their salary level. If this is the case, it needs to be rectified.

- Your pay is not competitive. Comparing to your peers in other companies in the same industry shows that you are paid less than they are. You need to do your homework to obtain the information and industry salary data to back your claim. Online resources such as Indeed.com or Glassdoor.com provide useful information on the salary compensation and benefits of different companies. However, this is a difficult sell because it's not a straightforward comparison. The HR manager would want to compare the total compensation package and not just the base salary. This includes, among other things, bonus, vacation days, stock incentives, 401K matching and health benefits. Because it's difficult to get accurate data from other companies to support your claim, this would be a tough hill to climb.

However unfair it may seem, companies usually are not inclined to change your salary in this case for a couple of reasons. One, your company already has a salary structure and as long as your job level's salary is within the designated range, there is no problem to be corrected. Secondly, if the company adjusts your salary for this reason, it may open up a can of worms for other employees in the company. As a result, it's unlikely your company will accommodate your request. The one situation your company might be more open to re-examine your salary is when you receive a better job offer from another company. That may be your best chance to negotiate a better salary. Refer to the "How to Negotiate a Job Offer" chapter for more details. Due to the need to hire strong employees, companies need to be competitive in their offer. This can create an undesirable situation where current employees are paid less than new employees in the same job level. Unfortunately, this is a fact of life. There may come a point where the only option you have to increase your salary significantly, outside of getting a promotion, is to look for a job with another company. When you receive a better offer from another company, you can decide whether to accept or use it to negotiate a better salary with your current company.

- You are paid lower than your peers in the same job level. An example of this is when a new employee joins the company with a base salary higher than yours even though that employee has the same job level as you. Unlike you, this employee has not contributed to the company; so it seems grossly unfair that you get paid less. Another example: a co-worker is doing a similar job and has the same performance ranking as you but received more pay raise than you. One likely reason for this is that her starting salary was higher than yours when she joined the company and the salary increase is a percentage of the base salary. While both cases have a reasonable argument, you're unlikely to be able to convince the company to make the changes. As I discussed earlier, employers compete for workers in the market place and at times they have to pay a high salary to get the candidates they want.

- Your salary increase was negatively affected because you were "unfairly" evaluated. It's best to prepare your manager to represent you fairly before he goes into the evaluation meeting with other managers. Or if the company evaluates employees individually, prepare your manager thoroughly before he sits down to review your performance. It's much more difficult to change the review outcome once the review results are completed. The one recourse you have is to convince your manager you deserve a better performance review outcome and to negotiate with him to make an exception and give you more of a salary increase than your review result allows. However, if you feel strongly about this and you're not getting satisfactory answers from your manager, you may want to escalate it to a higher management level. Your odds are long here, but I have seen a few cases that worked out in the employee's favour.

HOW TO APPROACH ASKING FOR A RAISE

You have done your homework and determined you have a strong case and want to move ahead. You should consider asking for a raise if you have confidence that your manager values your work and wants to keep you on his team. Think of this as a negotiation. Here is the approach to use in negotiating:

HOW TO ASK FOR A RAISE

1. Understand the true issues and parameters of the negotiation.

2. Assess where possible tradeoffs exist.

3. Determine your desired outcome and the walkaway value.

4. Make your best estimate of the other side's lowest value.

Let's apply this approach.

1. **Understanding the issues and parameters**. The issue here is clear. You want to negotiate for a salary raise and are equipped with information, rationale and data to support your case.

2. **Assess where possible tradeoffs exist**. From your perspective, think about possible tradeoffs you can make. Be creative. Instead of a raise, would you settle for stock options, a cash bonus or other non-monetary items such as extra vacation days, opportunities to attend popular industry conferences, or a new project that will give you more visibility? From your understanding of the manager and his flexibility, think about the possible areas he may be willing to compromise. You may not have a lot of insight here, so when you sit down to talk with your manager, ask questions to find out as much information as possible. This will help you think of potential options you can propose.

3. **Determine your desired outcome and walkaway value.** This is an important step. Based on all the information you have so far, think about these two values. The walkaway value is especially important to consider since you are willing to walk away if you get less than this outcome. To help you determine the walkaway value, think about the lowest outcome you would accept before you would be willing to look for another job. Let's assume that you are generally satisfied and like your job, the company and the people, and even if you didn't get what you wanted, you would be willing to stay put. In this case your walkaway value is status quo – no change to your current situation. Or you are willing to search for another job and join another company if you don't get some compensation above what you are currently getting. Give serious consideration to what your walkaway value is.

4. **Make your best estimate of the other side's lowest value**. If you don't really know, ask yourself questions that may give you some clue. Questions such as: "How much does your manager value you and your work?" and "How willing is he to lose you, and how hard would it be to replace you if you leave?" may give you some clue about his flexibility. If you believe that he doesn't value your work enough to try to keep you if you leave, then you may not want to go through with the meeting. On the other hand, if life would be really difficult for him if you leave, you have leverage here to negotiate since he's more likely to accommodate.

HOW TO ASK FOR A RAISE

When it's time to sit down with your manager, follow these steps:

- Explain to him that you have been putting your best effort into your job and contributing to the company as much as you can. You have given it a lot of thought and believe your salary is low and would like to request a raise. Here is an example of what to say: "I have been with the company for a while now and I have always given my best effort to contribute to the company. I have been giving my salary situation a lot of thought and I believe my salary is not competitive with the market and I would like to request a raise. Let me tell you why." Then give the manager the reasons, data, and any information from your research to support your case.

- Ask him for his thoughts. Listening to his comments will give you some ideas of where he stands. If he's open to your request and asks what you have in mind, be prepared to give him a percentage raise and explain why. If he says he has no flexibility, ask him to explain and then probe for areas where he may have more flexibility. Ask: "If it's not possible to give me a raise, which areas do you have flexibility?" and listen to what he comes up with. If you don't hear anything meaningful, ask: "Is giving stock incentives an option? Do you have any flexibility on that?" or "What about a cash bonus?" If he is open to these ideas and says he will check with HR, let him know you appreciate the effort and ask for a follow-up time. In general, if your manager values your work and wants to keep you, he will look for some ways to appease you, even if he cannot give you a raise or much else.

- Your objective of the meeting is to get closure or the next actionable step. The outcome of the meeting should be: (1) yes, your manager agrees and supports your request and will ask for approval; (2) no, there is nothing he can do or seems willing to do for you, which tells you where you stand; (3) he's open to consider your request but needs to look into it; or (4) he cannot give you a raise but is open to other ideas. Don't end the meeting until you are clear on the next step. Ask and clarify the next step if you're not sure, and confirm when he will follow up with you.

Even if you don't get your wish, your manager is likely to keep your request in mind, especially if your case has merit. At the next salary review time, he may be more flexible in giving a higher raise than he normally would, assuming that you get a decent performance review.

ADDITIONAL TIPS

- There are websites offering useful information about specific companies' salary compensations and benefits. For example, on Glassdoor.com, you can get information on a company's annual salaries as well as details on company benefits.

158

HOW TO ASK FOR A RAISE

- Don't use personal hardship or financial difficulties as justifications for your request, such as "I cannot afford to make ends meet or pay my bills," or "My husband is unemployed and I need to make more." Companies focus on business issues so you should focus on the business justifications.

- Don't be arrogant or give the impression that your case is so obvious, you should not even have to ask for a raise, or come across as "I am entitled to a raise". It's a real turn-off.

- Don't give an ultimatum or threat. It doesn't serve any purpose other than push your manager into a corner. If you do decide to use this tactic, be sure that you're ready to walk away.

- Don't lie. Don't make up stories or data you don't have in order to give yourself leverage. If you're caught with a lie, you will lose credibility and trust from your manager and it can hurt your case in the future. He will be less likely to give you the benefit of the doubt.

- Don't push past the limit and try to go for every dime you can get. If you can get something between your desired and walkaway value, consider taking it and not pushing it further. Keep in mind the adage "Penny wise, pound foolish".

About the Authors

Dennis Mark has more than 30 years of experience in the Information Technology industry, holding senior leadership positions including Vice President and General Manager of Solutions & Services for HP Inc Asia Pacific. In his international consulting capacity, he provides business subject matter expertise supporting organisational development, critical research and business decisions.

Michael Dam is an Adjunct Lecturer at Santa Clara University, California. He conducts career talks at universities as well as teaching career workshops, and provides individual coaching to career professionals. Michael holds an MBA and participated in the prestigious Accelerated Executive Leadership Program at Stanford University.

Dennis Mark and Michael Dam's 2022 publication, *Thriving At Work: What School Doesn't Teach You*, was lauded as "an absolute gem" and "a must-have career 101 handbook".